ASPIRE

3 POWERFUL STRATEGIES *for* CREATING

MORE *of* WHAT YOU WANT, NOW

OLE CARLSON

GREENLEAF
BOOK GROUP PRESS

Published by Greenleaf Book Group Press
Austin, TX

Distributed by Greenleaf Book Group LLC

For ordering information or special discounts for bulk purchases, please contact Greenleaf Book Group LLC at PO Box 91869
Austin, TX 78709, (512) 891-6100.

Design and composition by Greenleaf Book Group LLC
Cover design by Greenleaf Book Group LLC

Publisher's Cataloging-in-Publication Data

(Prepared by The Donohue Group, Inc.)

Carlson, Ole.
   Aspire : 3 powerful strategies for creating more of what you want, now / Ole Carlson. -- 1st ed.

   p. ; cm.

'The Dash,' p   c   Linda Ellis
(www.lindaellis.net) who owns & registered the
copywrite, may not be copied in any medium
without Ellis' written consent.

   ISBN-13: 978-1-929774-71-5
   ISBN-10: 1-929774-71-0

1. Success--Psychological aspects. 2. Success--Anecdotes. 3. Conduct of life--Psychological aspects. 4. Conduct of life--Anecdotes. 5. Self-actualization (Psychology) I. Title. II. Title: Aspire : 3 powerful strategies for creating more of what you want, now

BF637.S8 C27 2009
158/.1   2008941985

Part of the Tree Neutral™ program, which offsets the number of trees consumed in the production and printing of this book by taking proactive steps, such as planting trees in direct proportion to the number of trees used: www.treeneutral.com

Tree Neutral

Printed in the United States of America on acid-free paper

09 10 11 12 13 14   10 9 8 7 6 5 4 3 2 1

First Edition

CONTENTS

Dedication • v

Foreword   From New Orleans' Tough Ninth Ward
             to NFL Stardom by Marshall Faulk • vii

Acknowledgments • xi

Prologue   The Ultimate Reality Show—Your Life • xiii

STRATEGY 1: INVESTIGATE YOUR LIFE

CHAPTER 1   Your Fingerprints Are at Every Scene • 3

CHAPTER 2   Start Creating What You Want, Now • 19

CHAPTER 3   A Road to More • 43

CHAPTER 4   Conditioning the Innocent • 59

STRATEGY 2: ESTABLISHING THE FUNDAMENTALS

CHAPTER 5   Inside the Perimeter • 75

CHAPTER 6   Your Moon • 93

CHAPTER 7   Stay on Your Red Carpet • 111

CHAPTER 8   Creating More • 121

STRATEGY 3: THE MANIFESTATION TRILOGY

CHAPTER 9   The Trilogy: Saying More • 133

CHAPTER 10   The Trilogy: Seeing More • 141

CHAPTER 11   The Trilogy: Feeling More • 155

REVIEW

Epilogue   Tool Time • 179

DEDICATION

There is no beautifier of complexion, or form, or behavior, like
the wish to scatter joy and not pain around us. 'Tis good to give a
stranger a meal, or a night's lodging. 'Tis better to be hospitable to
his good meaning and thought, and give courage to a companion.
We must be as courteous to a man as we are to a picture, which
we are willing to give the advantage of a good light.

—RALPH WALDO EMERSON
AMERICAN ESSAYIST, POET, AND LEADER OF THE TRANSCENDENTALIST
MOVEMENT IN THE EARLY NINETEENTH CENTURY

This book is dedicated to Helen and Paul Cope, at the time of this
writing both ninety years young, having been married for sixty-seven
years and never having wavered in their love for one another or their
expression of love to me. Helen and Paul are healthy and vibrant and
show no signs of slowing down. My friends Susan and Steve refer to
them as the bionic couple. It is a perfect description, as the Copes
seem indestructible, with no apparent rust.

They start their day with a Tai Chi class followed by aerobic exercises. They are busy with golf matches, bridge tournaments, meals
to prepare, new restaurants to explore, and friends to visit and care
for. They do these things in their unique loving and caring manner. They've told me that they should have chosen younger friends
because many of their contemporaries are passing away, or simply
cannot keep up with them.

Helen and Paul maintain an active travel schedule visiting with
their adult kids and numerous grandchildren and great-grandchildren
scattered throughout the United States. Each night Helen and Paul
fall to sleep holding hands and renewing their love for one another.

They are truly remarkable and have influenced my life for the past six decades in ways that are difficult for me to comprehend. My fondest wish is that I may someday pay forward what they did for me to anyone who I can influence, inspire, and help transform to his or her next level. That is my personal mission. Most of the expert training I've received I learned and experienced from the Copes. You should meet them. You would be better off for it.

FOREWORD

FROM NEW ORLEANS' TOUGH NINTH WARD TO NFL STARDOM

BY MARSHALL FAULK

Buckle up. Get ready to ask yourself hard questions. Get ready to get clear about what you aspire to have more of. That is what Ole Carlson is encouraging us to seek in this remarkable book. His message is one of hope to improve our lives. He gives us the blueprint to obtain it.

Ole's message has resonated in my life. We have similar stories. We both had to overcome social and economic adversity to gain our success. We both came from blue-collar backgrounds with no silver-spoon handouts. We both wanted more out of our lives than what was immediately available.

I grew up the youngest of six brothers. My mother, Cecile, is a stubborn and self-determined woman. She had multiple jobs contributing to the family income. She is a proud and private person. I learned to be strong willed and determined from her. My dad, Roosevelt, was a truck driver. I would make deliveries with him. He was also part owner of a restaurant. I'd clean up at closing time. I learned a strong work ethic and to always have hope from him. My parents were my first influencers and established my foundation.

I grew up in the Ninth Ward Desire Projects in New Orleans. You could wind up in the wrong direction and take a life-altering turn. It was a battleground for drug dealers and criminals. Someone was killed there daily. Survival was most everyone's basic strategy. You had to cover your back. I learned to look out for myself. I had larger aspirations than to settle there. I wanted more.

In junior high school, sports entered my life and provided an opportunity for me to escape from the projects. In high school football, I played every position on offense but the offensive line, which was for the big guys. When the colleges recruited me, they wanted me to play defensive back. I wanted to play running back. That's where I belonged. San Diego State University gave me the opportunity. They started me at the number eight running back position. I had to be in the top three to stay. I knew that I could do it. I could see myself at the top of the rung. My goals were focused and I was determined. By the time the season started, I was the number two back and on my journey to the NFL.

I was drafted in 1994 by the Indianapolis Colts and remember the day I signed my first contract and how I felt. Wow! The questions from doubters came when I began to play in the NFL. Is Marshall big enough? Can he take the pounding? Can he break tackles? I never had those concerns. I set specific goals. I saw myself playing at the NFL level. I could feel it. I told myself every day that I could do it, that I was good enough. And I was.

We lost a lot of games early in my career. Focusing and setting goals helped me endure. I remembered the optimistic nature of my dad—the hope that he passed on to me. I was influenced by the determination that my mother role-modeled. By 1999, I was with the St. Louis Rams. In our first season together, we became Super Bowl champions.

The 2006 season would be my last in the NFL. It was time. Coaching changes were coming the following year, and I did not want to go through the football peaks and valleys. Injuries began to play a role. I turned to television and found joy as a commentator talking about the game I love. It made it easier for me to retire.

I had something to move toward that was more than I had. One day, I would love to manage an NFL team. As Ole suggests, I am reloading, resetting, and allowing the journey to continue by looking through the windshield instead of the rearview mirror.

My career and my life mirror many of the chapters in Ole's book. I had to be accountable. I needed to create a life that mattered and set a sound foundation for it to manifest. I had to establish and follow my vision. I defined a meaningful mission, one that was important to me. I was guided by the values that I learned from my parents, and I stayed with my goals. I affirmed and was affirmed in countless ways. I saw my future and felt the evolving success. It is a road map that I continue to follow. It is the one Ole lays out for you with detail and personal passion.

This book will help you get through your tough seasons. With a football in my hands, I was comfortable. I was doing what I was meant to be doing at that time in my life. Things are different now. I have another vision driven by familiar life-enhancing values. With this book in your hands, you are one step closer to your destiny—to a remarkable life that you can celebrate because you chose it. What do you aspire to have more of? What do you want to create in your life?

ACKNOWLEDGMENTS

No one who achieves success does so without acknowledging the help of others. The wise and confident acknowledge this help with gratitude.

—ALFRED NORTH WHITEHEAD
ENGLISH MATHEMATICIAN, PHILOSOPHER, AND AUTHOR

This book is a composite of what I've learned from most everyone who has entered and influenced my life. People have been working on and with me for six-plus decades. The scaffolding is still being erected in areas that need to be added, shored up, ripped out, repaired, or remodeled. The message and methodologies within the pages of *Aspire* are representative of my lifelong experience.

The first acknowledgment goes to a powerful, compact package—my wife, Sue Ann. She is my cornerstone. Sue Ann praises me when I'm remarkable and challenges me when I'm missing deadlines. She has made insightful and positive contributions to our book and seminar materials. She is courageous, resilient, tenacious, and intelligent. My wife thinks about topics differently than I do. She is right without being righteous—more often than my ego likes to admit. She is my relentless advocate and a superstar in her own right.

People and their teachings that have influenced my work and this book are Wayne Dyer, Brian Tracy, Scott Peck, Tim Gallwey, Lou Tice, Phil McGraw, Anthony Robbins, Rhonda Byrne, Helen and John Boyle, Nikki Nemerouf, Maxwell Maltz, and David Whyte. A special thanks goes to Marshall Faulk for the foreword, David Arvin for helping me work out the title, Dale Butler for his candid feedback, and Helen and Paul Cope for being the object of the dedication.

I apologize if I have used an idea or an exercise that I received from another without giving the appropriate acknowledgment. All that

I've learned—theories, insight from great teachers, and life-changing strategies—became ingredients in a whirling, swirling blender.

I would like, of course, to thank all of the dedicated and experienced people at Greenleaf Book Group for bringing this book to the market. They were professional, insightful, and responsive, and they elevated my writing to another level. It was my pleasure working with them on this book. Thank you all.

Finally, I want to thank all of you who have purchased *Aspire*. It is my hope that the following pages will inspire, influence, and transform each of you to your next level. I wish you well and a safe journey.

Ole Carlson
ole@influencemany.com

PROLOGUE

THE ULTIMATE REALITY SHOW—YOUR LIFE

Nothing splendid has ever been achieved except by those who dared [to]
believe that something inside them was superior to circumstances.

—BRUCE BARTON
ADVERTISING EXECUTIVE, RELIGIOUS WRITER, AND U.S. CONGRESSMAN

Don't accept that others know you better than yourself. Work
joyfully and peacefully, knowing that right thoughts and
right efforts will inevitably bring about right results.

—JAMES ALLEN
ENGLISH AUTHOR OF *AS A MAN THINKETH*

Many aspire to have more in their lives, but what is *more*? *More* is relative.
One person's mountainous goal may be just a slight rise on the horizon
for another. Lofty aspirations for me might be the bare minimum for
you. *More* seems to depend upon the perception of the seeker.

I am familiar with this premise. It hits home when I am looking
up from the short end of the stick and measuring where I am and
what I have achieved compared to the long-end-of-the-stick crowd.
I used to ponder that crowd and think: "I can't imagine how those
high-achieving folks can create such remarkable and consistent results.
They seem to have it all together and in balance." Can you visualize
remarkable outcomes in your life? Can you see yourself having more?
If you cannot, therein lies the problem, which we will explore as you
read the following pages. It could be that you have aspired to have
more, but obstacles were in your way. Obstacles such as you.

Many of the so-called self-proclaimed evolved suggest that everyone should be satisfied with what they currently have. They assert that there are no good or bad outcomes, only neutral ones. Everything in your life—both the positive and the negative results—is perfect. Events, circumstances, and situations simply exist, and you should quit evaluating. They claim that everything you have is what you need at this time in your life. To aspire to have more than what you have is egocentric, and it discounts your current perfect situation.

Personally, I find it difficult to consider and accept the tragedies, losses, and shortcomings in my life as being perfect, as being neutral. It irritates and confuses me to think that I should accept matters as they are, without attempting to change or, at the very least, to alter my response to these events. Someday I might take that elevated and seemingly passive view, but apparently I am not yet evolved enough to consider my life from that perspective.

I know that I am not supposed to compare myself to others. I understand that principle intellectually, but I find it difficult to avoid this constant temptation in our Western civilization. I compare myself with almost everybody. I bet you do, too. Comparisons do get personal and unavoidable if you remain awake, that is, noticing what is happening around you. The act of comparing then accelerates rapidly past the intellectual stage to the real question: Why do some have more of the good things in life and some do not? Why do some people aspire to achieve more and others remain either where they are or in a state of constant struggle—rationalizing or justifying their current state?

The choice is either to settle for what is or to do something about it. I have effective, easily accessible internal and external tools for you to use to make your life better and more fulfilling. I have a simple-to-read book to get you started on your journey to create a remarkable life that attracts more of what you want and deserve—more of what you aspire to. Get excited. It may not be cool to break a sweat. Go ahead, then, and just glow elegantly. But would you rather be cool and stagnant or warm and active? Because if you do get a little worked up and perspire, it may change your life for the better! *Pass me that cotton towel*, please.

I have been on both ends of the stick, short *and* long. Periods of an excellent life with extraordinary results have been interrupted by episodes of "this sucks" and "I think that I would rather kill the source of this misery than continue this self-imposed folly."

If I had my choice between the haves and the have-nots, I'd cast my vote with the haves and submit my adoption application to them. Or better yet, I'd learn how they got to where they are and enjoy the accompanying fruits of living a similar life. It's that "give 'em a fish or teach 'em to fish" routine.

Many people who grace the cover of *People* magazine—the haves—*appear* to have more fun, more leisure time, and more freedom to do what they please. They go wherever and whenever they desire, possess abundant resources, and stockpile ample reserves just in case they blow it. Let's be real: The haves simply have more of everything, and many do seem joyful, grateful, deserving, and able to handle the limelight with dignity in spite of the paparazzi who hound their every move.

There are exceptions, of course; having a profusion of tangible trinkets and celestial enlightenment does not always guarantee happiness. Trinkets and enlightenment may contribute to a happy life, so please don't disregard them. But balance is the key to total fulfillment. Consider the totality of your life by including loving relationships, excellent health, extensive travel, financial security, acceptance of other points of view, and other elements of your life that bring you joy. Be careful, objective, and courageous about what you are justifying just because you have secured it or it is easily within your grasp.

You can either have what you say is important to you or you can have all the reasons, excuses, and rationalizations why you cannot have it. You cannot have both.

I attended recently the annual conference of Vistage International, the world's leading chief executive organization, in Washington, D.C. Jack Canfield (of *Chicken Soup* series fame) was the featured keynote speaker. As he spoke, it was obvious he was proud of what he had overcome and accomplished in his professional and private lives. Canfield's road to fame and fortune was not a straight path sprinkled with rose petals and silver spoons. His success did not come on a platinum platter.

In explaining how he had arrived at his success, Jack projected upon multiple mammoth screens colored PowerPoint images of his tangible possessions. We viewed his expansive and expensive mansion on the shores of Santa Barbara. He showed us his Lexus that is waxed and detailed once a week. We saw a copy of the royalty check from his publisher: seven figures, stretched three feet high, made out to him!

Canfield is impressive, and I felt slightly envious and later ashamedly jealous. He seemed humble yet confident and grateful regarding what he had accomplished. It appeared he was happy and not suffering from any form of chronic guilt. His recent fame and fortune were not causing him any undue anxiety. It was quite perfect.

Observing him on stage and absorbing his message, I thought, *Good for you, Jack. Not bad. Could be me saying those things and showing those images to an audience as I keep making progress, both personally and professionally.* He provided me with a picture of what was to come as my career keeps moving along a similar track. We have somewhat comparable professional experiences; we're both authors, keynote speakers, seminar leaders, corporate trainers, and business gurus. Jack Canfield is just slightly ahead of me in his career, but the separation is slight. His message was tangible evidence of what might be in store for me if I keep doing what I've been doing and progressing at my current rate. I was inspired and encouraged.

Following his presentation, I facilitated a workshop with twenty people from his keynote audience. One of my participants, Kim, had a totally different experience of Jack than I did. She was appalled and somewhat indignant by what she claimed was Canfield's apparent lack of respect for the audience. She suggested that many attendees did not enjoy, possess, or place equal value on the toys that he had illuminated in his PowerPoint presentation. She was turned off by his blatant display of tangible wealth. She disliked his arrogant reference to himself and his self-promoting accomplishments. She disapproved of how he persisted in talking about what he possessed in a world that had so much need. Kim had enormous energy and a well-entrenched attitude supporting her point of view. Many others in the room did not experience it in that manner.

From all outward appearances, Kim is living a life entirely different from the one that Jack Canfield has created for himself and his family. She was resentful and appeared to be stuck in her self-assigned role in life. She spoke about how difficult it was to make her business successful. She was frustrated having to continually live on the edge financially. She wanted more out of life, but circumstances kept creating obstacles that prevented her from achieving the life she felt she deserved and desired. She was in the minority in a room of high-performing colleagues.

Two people can be in the same room, at the same time, listening to the same speaker, yet come away with two different interpretations. Why? Each person has a different point of view coming into the situation. The internal filter each carries with them determines what they will experience in the moment. What viewpoint and interpretation might have served Kim better and provided her with more options? How does this apply to your life? Let's explore.

What you focus on and obsess about tends to expand beyond its original dimensions and settle in your mind until you consciously reset it. What real chance does Kim have to experience abundance while she is reinforcing and holding firm to her scarcity mentality—that self-determined internal filter of lack and limitation? Jack Canfield was showing the audience the road map to the success that he had created. Kim insisted on filtering his message through her own self-limiting blinders. She defended her position by attacking him for what she lacks or fails to understand. She had the wrong target in the crosshairs and her finger on the trigger, willing to shoot an innocent victim. Some self-examination of her belief system, which was blocking her from finding more intangible-tangible balance in her life, would have served her better. I would suggest that she aspire to be more open, more accepting, and more willing to examine other points of view and other lifestyles.

Pay attention, for you might be doing something similar. What are your internal filters? Do they allow you to affirm, see, feel, and experience life? Are they accelerating you toward what you aspire to, or are they holding you hostage to what you have?

Be careful about having extraordinary energy, stamina, and opinions about a specific agenda. Examine what is driving that effort and creating the end results. Could that effort be a conscious or unconscious conspiracy to contribute to the threads of an elaborate tapestry of obstacles that you have hung up between you and what you aspire to? Here is the good news: You *can* remove the obstacles that you have built. You can tear down the entire structure by using intentional, conscious, and well-constructed consistent thoughts, mental pictures, and emotions. You *can* create outcomes that will bring you joy and gratitude and that will fulfill your egoless desires. You may have to release what you know. If something is not working, ask yourself why not? You *are* capable of learning new and more effective ways to have more of what you want if you are willing.

We are going to explore these questions and the process that will help you manifest what you enjoy and deserve to have. If it worked for me, it can work for you.

I am like many of you reading this book. I have had my low and fretful moments. I come from humble beginnings and find that life can be somewhat curly. I spent years trying to straighten it out my way, but with little sustained progress. I would enjoy brief moments of enlightened achievement interrupted by extended periods of setbacks and self-imposed correcting that led back to the familiar, yet unsatisfying.

Recently I spoke to a group of successful CEOs in Los Angeles, and after revealing my background and the difficulties I had encountered, one of the CEOs raised his hand and candidly said, with all good intentions: "Ole, I don't want you to take this the wrong way, but you are an inspiration. No kidding, you really are. I mean, hell, if you can do it, anyone can." I took it as a compliment.

Three decades ago, I understood the process intellectually and agreed philosophically with what we are about to explore. It's only recently, however, that I have applied the process with any degree of passion and commitment. The student was not prepared for the teacher to have a significant impact. An axiom old but true. We learn and make the right moves when we are ready. An accumulation of life experiences provides a platform from which we can go up the ladder. We can take shortcuts by being aware of and accountable for our lives, which I will cover in chapter 1. After I became ready and woke up to what was possible, the results were dramatic regarding mind, body, spirit, self, abundance, relationships, and balance.

More is relative. My life is substantially and measurably better than it was a decade ago. The long end of the stick is in sight. I hope it keeps extending because that indicates I am continuing to evolve—to become better and to improve in a joyful and grateful manner. Having more in my life did not happen by "just showing up," as comedian Woody Allen suggests, or by waiting for my turn.

There was no handout, no inheritance, and no intervention. There was no wealthy new trophy mate, no lottery, no retirement package, no trust fund, no adoption, and no looking back. The success that my wife and I are experiencing is not by accident. These results are intentional, provided by a loving and abundant Universe. I am in the midst of a work in progress, building brick by brick. I am happy and grateful for the advancement. There is still much more to do, be, and have. Areas of concern still exist, but what I do not have now is on its way. I am making myself worthy of and receptive to present and future gifts. The runway is being cleared and swept clean of self-imposed debris and obstacles. You must be willing to let go of what is not working and be in the present.

As you read each chapter, you will find a balance in the manifestation process between what are basically accepted principles of sound psychology and what are the beliefs of those who profess the vast power of the Universe and the Law of Attraction, recently brought to light by Rhonda Byrne in her book and DVD, *The Secret*. I am bolting them together. Stay engaged whenever you bump up against a statement or an opinion that is contrary or challenges one of your core conditioned beliefs. It is not an either-or proposition. The findings and concepts are not mutually exclusive of one another. Some occurrences are explained readily and have become known in the field of the behavioral sciences as "facts," while others remain a mystery even to the experts.

At the end of each chapter is a series of exercises and questions for you to address to anchor your learning and to propel you forward. Have fun. Stay open.

STRATEGY 1:

INVESTIGATE YOUR LIFE

CHAPTER 1

YOUR FINGERPRINTS ARE
AT EVERY SCENE

Each one of us has something no one else has . . . your fingerprints . . .
Be an individual. Be unique. Stand out. Make noise.
Make someone notice. That's the power of the individual.

—JON BON JOVI
AMERICAN MUSICIAN, SONGWRITER, AND ACTOR

You are accountable for your life. Nobody else is. Therefore, you need to align with who you are and refuse to be held hostage by what others want you to be, do, or have. You need to serve your best interest and not be constrained by a role that was assigned to you by someone else. You need to aggressively pursue what is important to you, and you need to pursue it rationally and with clarity.

Born into the Kennedy dynasty, Maria Shriver has spent a great deal of her life living up to her famous family's legacy and expectations. She is not only the niece of former President John F. Kennedy and Senators Robert and Ted Kennedy but also the first lady of California as the wife of Governor Arnold Schwarzenegger. That can be a heavy burden to live up to, and she admits that she acquiesced to surrendering her passion for her journalism career for the good of the family and the demands of NBC when Schwarzenegger became the governor of California. In October 2007, during a speech before a packed crowd at the annual California Women's Conference, Shriver made her stand in a confession of sorts. "As long as I was trying to anticipate what you wanted from me, as long as I was trying to fulfill other people's expectations, I was in a losing game, a game that I had been playing since I was a kid. That's what I want to focus on this morning . . . letting go of other people's expectations of you so you can own your own life, write your own story, and live your own legacy." She is on that journey at age fifty-two and revealing her thoughts in her latest book, *Just Who Will You Be?* It is a good book and you should read it.

In order to help keep true to herself, Shriver wrote a list of "Ten Things I Pledge to Myself," and she invites others to compose their own pledges. Her pledge is as follows:

1. I pledge to "show up" in my life as myself, not as an imitation of anyone else.

2. I pledge to avoid using the word "just" to describe myself. For example, I won't say, "I'm just a mother," "I'm just a student," or "I'm just an ordinary person."

3. I pledge to give myself 10 minutes of silence and stillness every day to get in touch with my heart and hear my own voice.

4. I pledge to use my voice to connect my dreams to my actions.

5. I pledge to use my voice to empower myself and others.

6. I pledge to serve my community at least once a year in a way that will benefit other people.

7. I pledge to ask myself, "Who am I? What do I believe in? What am I grateful for? What do I want my life to stand for?"

8. I pledge to sit down and write my mission statement.

9. I pledge to live my own legacy.

10. And I pledge to pass it on.

I want to own my own life, write my own story, and live *my* version of Maria Shriver's pledges. After I inhale my final breath, I want to then vanish, having been all used up. I cannot reach that final objective if I am numbed out, driven by an insatiable ego, or directing my life to solely benefit others.

When autopilot conditioning and wide-awake awareness intersect, I hope that the latter will prevail. A life of frustration awaits you if you allow a frightened ego, disheartened by what others have or do, to dominate as you wind down to a state of conformity and unfulfilled dreams.

Do not live in the darkened shadows of what could have been. Refuse to choose a life of quiet desperation and irreversible regret. Reject the notion of playing it safe for the sake of inheritance, acceptance, or obedience to others so that they might be comfortable, served, and justified. What are you choosing? What are you invested in being, doing, and having, and for what reason and rationalization? Pay attention and be an active detective investigating your life. Your fingerprints are on all of your results.

Take care of yourself first with good intent. You can take care of others better from a foundation of strength rather than when your feet are mired in quicksand and you are being sucked down into a subservient life. You deserve more from life than finding in your final moments that your shackled hands are reaching desperately toward the surface for what might have been, but never will be.

Many are laid to rest with their dreams entombed along with them beneath chiseled headstones. Or the cooled gray ashes of what their lives might have been are scattered ceremoniously on fickle winds or outgoing tides. Eulogies are read commemorating what the departed achieved rather than what they held in abeyance. Time-stamped achievements often pale in comparison to the untapped potential that passes unnoticed along with the deceased. Grieving friends and family are left wondering who might be the next to leave undeclared hopes and desires behind. Don't let this happen to you. You deserve better. Take a stand for your life. Do it now! There is no other time to create your future.

The passing of those you care deeply about can be the wake-up call that alerts you to what you want more of. Your mortality clock will stop ticking one day, its hands idle. Science, medicine, and positive thinking have slowed the process, but they cannot end the inevitable fate of all human beings. It is up to you to learn from what is happening in your life and take appropriate action now. Are you up to it?

Wake up. Be aware. The only future you are assured of is this moment. Resist the mind-numbing, habitual herd mentality. Stop the obedient penguin march back to established and traditional patterns. Escape from the perceived safety of bordered comfort zones. End the erroneous thinking that someday you will get to what is essential to you. "Ah, someday I'll . . ." Someday is *always* too late.

The following line from *Les Misérables* warns us about the danger of conformity, falling in love with what we know rather than exploring what is outside of our comfort zone on a different path. "The common herd is like an old Narcissus, who adores himself and applauds the common." The herd mentality allows you to see only what is immediately in front of you. Self-inflicted blinders make you unaware of other life-enhancing possibilities that might lie just off the beaten path. You might miss an unexpected opening as the ritual of predictability, familiarity, and conformity continues to dominate your life and keep you on the straight and narrow. Many fail to seize this opportunity, and the ritual continues. Break the cycle. You cannot steer or accelerate your transformation while the car is on autopilot, directing your thoughts, mental pictures, and emotions. Biding time as your mortality clock ticks away is commonplace. Be uncommon.

SKIRT THESE ROADBLOCKS

Research shows that we create self-imposed obstacles that block us from what we aspire to have. Dr. Scott Peck, for example, suggests two such roadblocks in his landmark self-help book *The Road Less Traveled*: life is difficult, and people are lazy. These two inhibitors govern our potential, and in the end, they stimulate unbearable regret.

Life Is Difficult

Dr. Peck writes, "Life is difficult. This is a great truth, one of the greatest truths. It is a great truth because once we truly see this truth we transcend it. Once we truly know that life is difficult—once we truly understand and accept it—then life is no longer difficult. Because once it is accepted, the fact that life is difficult no longer matters." Stuff happens; no one is spared from having an impaired day. Loved ones succumb to cancer, subprime mortgages default, and seemingly solid marriages dissolve. The evening news reports that a massive hurricane has destroyed an entire city. Young men and women are sent to the Middle East to fight a war that seems impossible to win. We place our dreams on hold when the latest unforeseen drama of life interrupts them. It seems anything can happen.

Position, status, or yesterday's success is not a firewall that can protect anyone from experiencing adversity. The haves and the have-nots are all potential targets for what can go wrong in life. Adversity is an equal opportunity offender; it does not discriminate, no matter who you are, what you have achieved, or how many titles you hold. We are all vulnerable.

A paradox comes into play with successful, proactive people: They increase the odds of experiencing difficulties in life by not sitting on the sidelines. They deliberately place themselves in the bull's-eye of life. What separates them from less successful people is how they respond to the speed bumps and move on to whatever is next.

Achievement-oriented people do not remain stuck in the negative past or paralyzed by the current drama. Television legend Merv Griffin, who recently lost his long battle with prostate cancer, said: "You have to be constantly turning the page, which prevents me [*sic*] from getting caught up in any negativity. I just keep moving and enjoy the ride."

Griffin and other successful people find looking through the windshield at what lies before them to be more interesting than fiddling with the rearview mirror and dwelling on the ground they have already covered. High-achieving people have a curious forward approach to life; they want to explore what is next. They focus on what lies ahead and thus are not blinded by any bright approaching headlights reflected in the rearview mirror. Satchel Paige, legendary pitcher of the Negro baseball leagues, joked: "Don't look back. Something might be gaining on you." That something gaining on you might be an element of your past that has restricted your open-ended potential and has sentenced you to a no-growth life.

You cannot outrun the past if you keep focusing on it. Do not let your life be defined by sentences ending with a period. I encourage you to repeatedly insert a comma and the word "and" or the phrase "to be continued." Doing this will help you keep moving ahead.

In his book *The 10 Dumbest Mistakes Smart People Make and How to Avoid Them*, Dr. Arthur Freeman writes the following: "It doesn't make any difference whether what you face is something that affects your work, your personal relationships, your sense of security, your appraisal of self-worth, or your appearance . . . the way you think about your situation largely determines whether you will do anything about it and what you will do." Yes, life can be difficult. What are your thoughts regarding any current difficulties? Are you considering options, or are you tightening the noose?

People Are Lazy

The second roadblock Dr. Peck identified—people are lazy—is especially true when it comes to making changes in our lives. He writes, "Please keep in mind that some of the hardest-working people are 'lazy' when it comes to changing. It is fear that keeps us from changing. Fear that keeps us from doing the hard work that change requires." Fear is mostly an illusion that shackles us to what we have rather than what we aspire to. It is a veil as thick or as thin as we imagine it to be. The veil of fear needs to be swept aside or penetrated so that we can experience the treasures that await us on the other side.

It takes conscious, focused effort and courage to challenge an unreasonable boss and risk receiving harsh feedback. It takes guts to enter life-changing therapy, to leave a destructive codependent relationship, to lose all that weight once and for all, and to revitalize a dormant marriage. It is difficult until you realize the new and better results. It is difficult until you allow better outcomes to shape your tomorrow.

Winners in life still experience fear, but they make the effort to move beyond the obstacles. They focus on what is on the other side of the barricade rather than on the obstruction. Unabashed courage is acknowledging that you are afraid, that your knees are shaking, that your mouth is bone dry, that your thoughts are scattered. In spite of all that, you choose to move through the discomfort to the desired outcome, with no guarantee of success. Many people are lazy and will settle for what is instead of what *could be*, what is predictable versus what is mysterious, what is convenient and comfortable versus what might stretch and expand their world. Are you being lazy about a challenge confronting you, or are you being courageous?

AVOID THESE HAIRPIN TURNS

Other obstacles may impede your journey to fulfillment and stall your progress. Two of them are actually just flip sides of the same coin: fear of failure and fear of success.

Fear of Failure

Fear of failure paralyzes many goal seekers. What if you declare a goal, do your best, and fail to reach it? What will people think of you? What will you think of yourself? The default position is to play it safe and return to the familiar, to let today be similar to yesterday and tomorrow be a footprint of today. There is no apparent risk in that plan.

The fear-of-failure crowd will provide you with abundant support as they, too, seek support for taking such a stagnant stance in life. It often boils down to either doing things right or doing the right thing. Conformists who are shackled by the chains of fear of failure suggest that doings things right is the proper path to take. It involves little risk. This approach to life demands that the implementers make numerous small decisions that have little impact. These same implementers are confined within tight comfort zones as they adhere to the norms of the tribe. It is a conservative "don't rock the boat" approach that governmental and business bureaucracies thrive on.

Those who choose to do the right thing, on the other hand, support the notion that the implementer will make only a few decisions, but the impact of those choices will be significant and will lie outside the boundaries of traditional conformity. Entrepreneurs, free thinkers, and risk takers dominate this crowd. Which crowd do you want cheering you on?

William Shakespeare wrote, "Our doubts are traitors, and make us lose the good we oft might win, by fearing to attempt." Dr. Maxwell Maltz, plastic surgeon and author of *Psycho-Cybernetics*, similarly states, "Often the difference between a successful man and a failure is not one's better abilities or ideas, but the courage that one has to bet on his ideas, to take a calculated risk, and to act." I encourage you to act. Turn whatever you are thinking, picturing, and feeling into a remarkable reality. Calculate and wade confidently and intentionally out to the deeper regions of your life. Be an explorer, not a settler.

Renowned poet David Whyte of Yorkshire, England, told an audience that I was a part of in San Diego that the territory is much larger than the maps that we have for it. I encourage you to go beyond the horizon.

When famous Early American explorer Daniel Boone was asked by a Washington socialite if he had ever been lost in the wilderness, he replied, "No ma'am, but I have been a might bewildered for a month or two." Go explore; get lost temporarily. You will find your way, and in that exploration you might discover who you really are and what you truly aspire to have. You might learn to trust your choices over the choices made for you by others.

You needn't plunge initially off the high dive into uncharted waters, however, risking everything. Quantum leaps can be intimidating, as well as an unconscious strategy to sabotage yourself. Rather, I encourage you to begin by thinking bigger than you normally do, eventually thinking LARGE, far beyond where you are. You be the judge of what works for you. It is your life, and no one knows you better than you. George Bernard Shaw suggests that "Life isn't about finding yourself. Life is about creating yourself." Create what brings you joy and gratitude. Go ahead and stretch until the stretch feels normal, and then stretch further.

If you are reading this book, there is a high probability that you have had numerous successes. Set your aspirations and climb to the next level. Propel yourself to where your heart, your spirit, and your longings push and pull you.

Fear of Success

Another obstacle men and women face is the fear of success. President Theodore Roosevelt once said, "It is hard to fail, but it is worse never to have tried to succeed." It seems counterintuitive that anyone would be frightened of bettering his or her life. But many people are.

What if you luck out, reach the goal, and others expect you to repeat your recent success? What if you reach the objective and cannot sustain what you have achieved because deep down you know that you don't deserve what you accomplished? Both of those reasons seem to underlie the finding in a recent article in *Investment News* that nearly *one-third* of state lottery winners seek some sort of bankruptcy relief. How does that happen? The money was handed to them and they essentially consciously or unconsciously handed it back by squandering or mismanaging it, perhaps out of the fear of success.

What if you end up sabotaging what you obtained, and the interior demons of low self-esteem whisper to you: "I told you so. You should have played it safe. You should have returned to what was familiar, what you know. Who do you think you are?" Those who fear success are immobilized by innumerable "What if?" questions. Don't let the unknown rule your actions.

The fear of success has many masters. Dr. Denis Waitley, author, productivity consultant, and motivational speaker, states, "Procrastination is the fear of success. People procrastinate because they are afraid of the success that they know will result if they move ahead now. Because success is heavy, carries a responsibility with it, it is much easier to procrastinate and live by the 'someday I'll' philosophy." That "someday I'll" philosophy can migrate unconsciously to another column with the heading "what if I had only," and then it is too late. Your clock stopped ticking. Unless you were a one-time, paid-in-advance, credit-card-on-file new patient of Dr. Jack Kevorkian (he has no repeat patients) pacing nervously back and forth in his reception area waiting for your name to be called, few know when that moment will arrive—but it assuredly will.

DON'T TAKE THIS DETOUR

Families and cultural codes can sometimes lead us on a detour and thus discourage us from achieving and exceeding established norms. I grew up in such a family.

Ah, the luck of the draw, or maybe it's a celestial covenant in action. When I was an innocent young boy, my troubled father, whose life took a tragic and unrecoverable turn, scolded me frequently when he sensed I was contemplating or achieving what was no longer possible for him. Scowling with frustration, he often reprimanded me after enduring a difficult day with the words, "Young man, who do you think you are to try to do better in life than I have done?" It was an imposing question. It was also an unconscious command that I took seriously, so much so that my success was delayed until later in my life, after my father was gone. The bar was low, but it was the only bar I knew.

In my early adult years, I struggled with my self-esteem and my conditioned core beliefs about money and family. It was difficult and confusing to go against the commands of my parent and the role that had been assigned to and accepted by me. It had a firm grip on me. Lyman Carlson was not being cruel intentionally. He simply chose to drift asleep and erase a once positive and possible vision of his future. I was too young to sort it all out. He was too unaware and lost in his own despair to make better choices.

Much later, as an adult, I attended a Father's Day service at Unity Church in Bellevue, Washington. In a crowded pew, shoe-horned between other dads and their families, I listened to inspirational speaker Bob Trask preach to his attentive audience, "Fathers come and go, and when they go, they leave the very best of them in you."

What? That's not possible, I thought, fighting back the notion and the unexpected flow of tears. I had never entertained such an idea. I rejected the concept at first, but the words and the emotion would not disappear. They remained with increased intensity, pounding away at my awareness, dismantling what I had constructed for years. The light came on and there was no turning back. *What if Bob Trask is right, and I am wrong?* I had invested for so long, and with such devotion, in being the blameless victim, the underachiever with vast untapped potential. It was the story that I had created for myself, and I had assigned a supporting role to my father. This was now a defining moment that changed how I viewed myself and my relationship with my father. There was no turning back. Shame descended over me. I felt diminished.

For years, I had blamed Lyman outwardly and unconsciously for my shortcomings. I had many. But it had never occurred to me to include him in my numerous victories. He was my convenient scapegoat. I consistently justified and rationalized my latest setback in life by placing the fault on his burdened shoulders. It was all one-sided. Silence from his pauper's grave was his only defense.

Through Bob Trask's short, illuminating sentence I was able to understand and to acknowledge the gifts that my father had left inside of me. I started to count the numerous Lyman deposits that had influenced me since day one: my love of music, my athletic ability, my sense of humor, my spontaneous emotions, and my intelligence.

I had sentenced my father unjustly for the negatives. And until that moment, I had rejected the concept that *I* was accountable for my life. In the shift of my consciousness, my father went from being scapegoat to contributor. He and I assumed new roles as I became more aware. *Lyman, can you hear me?*

Are you blaming anyone unjustly for what is not working in your life? It is a serious query that deserves your thoughtful consideration. You can blame, rationalize, and justify, or you can choose to reconcile. Please choose the latter! What is your long-term payoff for making another the fall guy for your shortcomings? How long are you willing to hold that person and yourself hostage? As long as you do, he or she remains in control and you remain the helpless victim, the willing martyr, stuck in your current role. When will you be willing to own your results? Who is perpetuating and collaborating with you on that strategy, and for what selfish justification?

TAKE A NEW ROUTE

If life is difficult and people are lazy, and if the other obstacles that prevent people from living the life they aspire to are valid, many people will choose to remain stuck. Stagnancy strategies require effort, but the effort is familiar. It is a self-induced trance that becomes acceptable and an established comfort zone.

Faced with new and different approaches, people will choose what they know even though the results are not what they want. They continue to settle for familiar yet negative repetition. They remain in their assigned roles faithfully fulfilling the wishes of others and ignoring their own longings and desires. They stumble through life semiconscious; they continue either their downward spiral or their life of stagnancy.

That path is the road most traveled. It is an outcome that you do not deserve to create, but it might be a choice that you are making. Yes, I said *choice*. In the words of William Jennings Bryan, "Destiny is not a matter of chance, it is a matter of choice; it is not a thing to be waited for, it is a thing to be achieved."

For many people the choice concept is new or unfamiliar. Victimization, martyrdom, and being stuck in a role are seldom mentioned in the same breath with making intentional, conscious, life-enhancing choices. If it is your choice to remain stuck, then accept your decision and go about your business. At the end of any given day, you have either created value or waste. "The loving person is a person who abhors waste—waste of time, waste of human potential. How much time we waste, as if we were going to live forever," lamented author and former University of Southern California professor Leo Buscaglia.

In his hit song "Man in the Mirror," entertainer Michael Jackson states that if you want to make the world a better place, to make a difference, to make it right, and to feel real good, start with the man in the mirror. Start with yourself. Take a look at yourself and make a change.

It is ultimately up to you to take ownership for your life, to create the life that you desire. It is ultimately up to you to objectify and see the obstacles in your way for what they really are. It is ultimately up to you to correct whatever needs to be corrected because it is preventing you from having more of what you aspire to have now. It is ultimately up to you to take a new route. The tools for doing that are in the following chapters.

EXERCISES

Please purchase a journal in which to start recording your thoughts, insights, aha's, and intended actions as you read this book. It will assist you in organizing this material and allow you to interpret this information in your voice and in your style. You can also record these insights on your computer or PDA. Those devices are less personal and kinesthetic, but the world is changing. Do what works for you. Do not set limits for yourself. Seek balance and begin by answering the following questions in your journal.

- How do you want to **be** in your life? Common answers include being more open-minded, being more peaceful, and being a better listener.

- What do you want to **have** in your life? Usually people say something tangible, such as owning a mountain cabin, having financial freedom, or being in better health.

- What do you want to **do** in your life? Possibilities include floating down the Colorado River through the Grand Canyon, enjoying a glass of wine in a small bistro on the Champs-Élysées in Paris, or reading two books a month.

- What do you want to **start** in your life? Maybe it's spending more quality time with your family, getting more exercise, or investing in mutual funds.

- What do you want to **stop** in your life? Focus on things that do not serve you or others, such as smoking, working too hard, and being broke.

- What do you want to **continue** in your life? Focus on things that are working, such as learning, being a loving parent, and contributing to your community.

CHAPTER 2

START CREATING WHAT YOU WANT, NOW

Don't let yesterday use up too much of today.

—CHEROKEE INDIAN PROVERB

If you are coming from a position of spirit and not from one of ego-inspired, got-to-have-it-all greed, if you want more in life, and if you are willing to do the work, read on. It takes awareness and courage. Quit complaining about the negative conditions that you might have created. Leave whatever does not serve you in the past where it belongs. Overachiever Rocky Balboa summed it up perfectly in *Rocky IV* when he said, "I guess what I'm trying to say is, if I can change, and yous can change, everybody can change." You can change too, if you are willing.

Right now is the only time that you have to create what you aspire to be, do, and have. Don't hesitate! Accomplished musicians suggest that great music originates and is played between the notes: not the previous notes, not the following notes, but now. Eastern philosophy claims that pure creativity occurs in the gap between thoughts: not the previous thoughts, not the following thoughts, but now. Metaphysicians declare that everything you could reasonably want in life is within your grasp, or it is on its way now.

Actor Anthony Hopkins once said, "Today is the tomorrow that I worried about yesterday." Why worry? It is such a waste of time and focus, and it places limitations on your future. I would like to change that quote to read, "Today is the tomorrow that I consciously and intentionally created yesterday." The only time that you can count on is now. Stay conscious and orchestrate the today that you desire and deserve.

From *Idylls from the Sanskrit* comes this wise teaching:

THINK NOBLE THIS DAY

Think Noble This Day
For it is life
The life of life.
All is there
In its brief moment
All the reality
All the truth of existence
The joy of growth
The splendor of action
The glory of strength . . .
For yesterday he is but a dream
And tomorrow but a vision
But today, well lived
Forms each yesterday

Into a memory/dream of happiness
And each tomorrow
Into a vision of hope/realization of trust.
Thus, live this day with honor/confidence.

The Sanskrit teachings reinforce the notion of living in the now. Right now is the only time we can fulfill our dreams and truly experience what we aspire to have. Live each moment fully with joy and gratitude because this moment is the only one you have until the next moment comes—if it does. You will learn how to turn that creative switch on in the following chapters. First, you must become aware of everything that you aspire to. Then, you must commit with intention, joy, and gratitude to making those aspirations reality. Are you willing to do the work and receive the rewards?

You are surrounded by abundance. The limited-pie theory is wrong. Taking one slice for yourself does not leave less for others. Dr. Stephen Covey, author of *The Seven Habits of Highly Effective People*, suggests, "People with a scarcity mentality tend to see everything in terms of win-lose. There is only so much, and if someone else has it, that means there will be less for me." But that scarcity mentality is a fear-inspired concept. Whatever you take and gain for yourself will be replenished. You are not being selfish by participating in the inexhaustible abundance. There is enough for everyone. It is time to become wealthy in your bank account, your career, your spiritual life, your personal interests, your health, your relationships—all the aspects of a fulfilling and remarkable life.

Wake up! Put in motion your purpose, your dreams, your values, and your vision. Prioritize them ahead of the ceaseless chatter and noise of life that capture your time, attention, and energy. I once heard *consciousness* defined as "that annoying time between naps." Open your eyes to what is happening to your life and what you are attracting and creating. Be annoyed! It is a catalyst for transformation.

Make it a daily task to create a list of priorities. Sort your list by what is vital to your life rather than by things that define you externally, such as due dates. Do not let people invade your life and priorities without your permission. It is your life. Take control. Take back what you have given away! Where do you want to make a substantial deposit instead of passively standing by and letting others make withdrawals from you?

Not long ago I participated in a workshop for employees who continually allowed others to make withdrawals from them. They had accepted the role of victim. I was hired to teach these employees of a major high-tech organization on the East Coast how to run effective meetings. The accounting department calculated that the company wasted millions of dollars annually conducting unproductive meetings. The participants wandered reluctantly into the classroom, suspicious of what I was going to ask them to do. They probably felt management was forcing yet another corporate training on them. They did not see the training as a deposit; rather, they viewed the meeting as an unsolicited interruption and therefore another withdrawal from their already busy professional lives.

My first request was that the participants turn off the Palm, Treo or iPhones they each had strapped, pistol-like, to their belts. They were appalled and refused for fear of missing a summons from a superior to perform some immediate task. Theirs was a corporate culture—fostered and reinforced by executive leadership—that I was unable to unravel. The human resources director and the leadership team were conspicuously absent from the training. They and their direct reports never understood that the reason their meetings were ineffective was their refusal to turn off the interruptions and concentrate on important business. The employees in many ways had colluded with their leaders in allowing this withdrawal victim culture to continue. Complaining and blaming others became the norm instead of creating suitable solutions to their nonproductive meetings.

Most to-do lists focus on what others deem you should do. You find yourself droning through yet another day without significant evolution, transformation, or personal satisfaction. I suggest that you create a never-ending series of lists that capture the defining moments in your life. Benchmark your days signifying their relevance to *you*. In the movie *Tin Cup*, Kevin Costner, playing the role of washed-up pro-golfer Roy McAvoy, says, "When a defining moment comes along, you can do one of two things. Define the moment, or let the moment define you." You make the call. It is your life. Will you write the definitions for your life, or will you let others write your story?

Many of you have the means and the talent to create high-achieving, goal-oriented lives. Make certain that what you are creating is meaningful to you. "In order to do what really matters to you, you have to, first of all, know what really matters to you," says Dr. Edward Hallowell, psychiatrist and founder of The Hallowell Center. What are you waiting for? What is preventing you from declaring what matters?

NO EXCUSES

There is no exact moment or perfect place to declare that it is *your turn* in whatever hierarchical structure you chose to participate in, be it a family, business, society, or whatever. If you are waiting for conditions to be perfect, you are being foolish and wasting time. People invest considerable energy and time coming up with reasons, rationalizations, and excuses to postpone their rightful time to be next in line. That is a turnstile mentality. You deserve more than just obediently shuffling along. Get proactive, stand tall, reach up, and pull down your number from the dispenser on the wall. Hold that number high above your head, shout it out, and elbow your way—gracefully, I might suggest—to the front of the room. Be number one. The view is fantastic. Would you rather be the lead dog on a team in the Iditarod Trail Sled Dog Race or several rows back in the pack, where all you can see and smell is the . . . well, you get the idea.

A life dominated by routine and habit interferes with this self-actualization buzz. It boils down to making better choices, and it is time that we all start to choose consciously and stop "shoulding" on ourselves.

Howard Schultz, founder and CEO of Starbucks Coffee, suggests in his book *Pour Your Heart into It* that to seek true self-actualization one might

> *Care more than others think wise.*
> *Risk more than others think safe.*
> *Dream more than others think practical.*
> *Expect more than others think possible.*

By now most everyone is familiar with the story of how, with a wide-awake Schultz at the helm, Starbucks became an enormous international success after starting as the small Starbucks Coffee, Tea, and Spices store in Seattle's Pike Place Market in 1971. Pouring his care, risk taking, dreams, and expectations into Starbucks Coffee Company, it grew to a global force of 16,000-plus stores located in forty-four countries with 170,000 partner employees.

Just as familiar is the news that Schultz's company is now experiencing competition from unusual suspects, and he is rising to the challenge and implementing difficult and courageous decisions. High performers have challenges to meet; they always have a "next." They are flexible and continually reinvent themselves.

As Schultz suggests, let's start caring, risking, dreaming, and expecting more from our lives than we have been conditioned to believe is proper and acceptable. I often wonder why folks are so concerned about what others think. As author Ethel Barrett points out, "We would worry less about what others think of us if we realized how seldom they do." Disappointing, isn't it? You being the center of another person's Universe is not in the celestial cards. If you are, then it is probably not a healthy relationship.

THE UNIVERSE

I use the term "Universe" to refer to the entity that creates—or assists in delivering to you—more in your life. It can be a deity, an energy, a force, a belief, or a faith. The Universe is whatever you deem your higher power to be. It can be a spiritual, metaphysical, mystical, traditional, or fundamental religious doctrine. It can even be something tangible that has meaning to you. I am not concerned about labeling and defining what the Universe actually is. Who really knows or has the authority? Naming it tends to confine what the Universe is able to do and separates the 6.3 billion people inhabiting this planet. I do not care if you access the Universe through prayer, meditation, worship, positive thinking, or goal setting. What I do care about is recognizing that we are connected to a greater power that is available to us through whatever means we believe to be our truth. Whether or not you attribute the results in your life to a greater power is your business. The question that you need to objectively ask yourself is whether whatever you believe in and devote yourself to is working or not.

Many of you are doing great and living a life that suits you. You custom designed it. You have put into motion techniques, philosophies, and core belief systems that attract abundance, loving relationships, excellent mental and physical health, learning, and self-satisfaction. You have created a relationship with the Universe that is expansive and contributory. You remain open to the infinite possibilities of life. Wonderful! Let's see if we can expand what you are doing. Let's make the techniques that you are using visible, add a wrinkle or two to keep you evolving, and share what you know with others. You have made the choice to remain vertical, upright, and in motion. Congratulations!

For those of you who have not yet reached this point, what you are about to read and digest may be revolutionary; it may challenge family and cultural norms. As you read and grow, you may clash with religious dogma or challenge your past ways and violate tribal taboos. Those around you may question what you are doing. If they aren't inspired by you, you may wish to leave some of them behind where they have chosen to remain—stagnant.

The National Geographic Channel airs a weekly program called *Taboos*, which looks at how what is acceptable to you may be a taboo to others. The program highlights and explores different points of view from all geographical, sociocultural, and philosophical aspects of the planet. Watch it. You might learn something other than what your ancestors have conditioned you to believe is the absolute truth. If you do not consider outside points of view, you have chosen to remain horizontal.

Simply asking the question "Who has the ultimate answer?" may go against everything you were conditioned and taught to believe to be true. It takes courage to ask it, but you must if you are feeling stuck and wondering "Is this all there is?" What you are doing may not be working at the level you desire. There is an unfulfilled longing that will not go away. What is the source of this unrest? Where does this questioning and dissatisfaction come from? That quiet, intuitive voice inside that you know and have learned, or will learn, to trust will answer, "No. This is not all there is. There is more. Much more."

Indeed, there is much more waiting for you. The Universe is ready and willing to provide you with more of what you aspire to have.

If you sense this unrest, challenge your thinking and the manner in which you are approaching your life. Stay open to new ways of living a life that you can enjoy from a multidimensional and multilevel experience. Remember, the last nine words of any stagnant life are "This is the way I have always done it."

Self-help gurus preach that nobody is right or wrong and nobody is superior or inferior. Some suggest that we are all uniquely perfect and doing the best we can with our present level of awareness. Baloney! This notion lets people off the hook, allowing them to continue to be dominated by habitual mistakes and shortcomings. This philosophy grants them refuge from transformation or, at the very least, honest reflections in an objective mirror.

In my life, I have made choices when I knew I was not doing the best that I could with my level of awareness. I was acting irresponsibly. I intentionally chose to go ahead, creating poor results. Those are called mistakes. I have regrets. I cannot change what has happened in the past, but I can avoid making the same negative and negligent choices again. What choices are you justifying that do not serve you or others? How honest are you being with yourself? As I pointed out in the previous chapter, are you blaming someone else for your behavior? Please look in the mirror and reflect!

Life is a continuous and—hopefully—happy journey of conscious thinking and making choices that involves a series of next moments. That is what I wish for you. What do you want your next moment and choice to be? What are you thinking consciously about that will improve your life? Are you still smoking cigarettes and chewing tobacco? Do you overeat? Do you eat unhealthy foods? Do you forget to tell your loved ones that you love them? Have you decided to stop learning? When did you last have a doctor's physical, bring flowers home to your wife or husband, take your son or daughter out on a date, or become more skilled at your job? What do you want more of, and what do you aspire to start, stop, or continue?

I have no idea where you are on your journey. What is important to me is that you are a fellow traveler and you have a desire to experience more. I hope that nobody has told you that this material will be good for you, or that you need to read this book. If they have, put it down. Come back later when it is appropriate to do so and it is your choice.

I want your journey to be blissful. American comparative mythology and religion professor, lecturer, and writer Joseph Campbell suggests that you

> Follow your bliss. If you do follow your bliss, you put yourself on a kind of track that has been there all the while waiting for you, and the life you ought to be living is the one you are living. When you can see that, you begin to meet people who are in the field of your bliss, and they open the doors to you. I say, follow your bliss and don't be afraid, and doors will open where you didn't know they were going to be. If you follow your bliss, doors will open for you that wouldn't have opened for anyone else.

Let's go open doors and be happy and grateful for the riches that we discover beyond them.

THE LAW OF ATTRACTION

The Law of Attraction is a powerful, universal, self-fulfilling energy that is defined as the principle "like attracts like" applied to conscious desire. That is, a person's thoughts (conscious and subconscious), emotions, and beliefs cause a change in the physical world that attracts positive or negative experiences that correspond to the aforementioned thoughts, with or without the person taking action to attain such experience. A person's thoughts (conscious and unconscious), mental pictures, emotions, beliefs, and actions are said to attract corresponding positive or negative experiences, or harmonious vibrations of the Law of Attraction. In other words, you get what you think about; your thoughts determine your experience.

Focusing on the Law of Attraction, Rhonda Byrne's *The Secret* has enjoyed phenomenal worldwide success. It is perched prominently at the top of respected best-seller lists. It has been accepted, praised, and validated wholeheartedly by numerous well-known international celebrity endorsers and experts. Others who have equally impressive credentials have fiercely criticized Byrne's thesis, claiming there is no scientific evidence that the Law of Attraction is valid or worthy of further consideration. They believe that it is a sham and that her teachings are rabble-babble, new-age psycho-pop nonsense. Controversy surrounds the topic. Experts are challenging the opinions expressed, as well as the knowledge and credentials of the author and her supporters.

I can only evaluate my own experience and what works or does not work for me. My encounter of life is consistent and in alignment with the premise of *The Secret*. I believe that I have experienced and continue to experience the Law of Attraction. A number of events have occurred in my life that, frankly, I do not understand cognitively, nor am I able to explain rationally. Let me share just two such events to illustrate my point.

In the autumn of 1981, while living in Seattle, I organized a reunion of my 1961 high school football team. I invited the team to my home for a weekend to pay tribute and say farewell to James, our former teammate who was dying of a malignant brain tumor. On my list of thirty people to call was Tom, who I had lost contact with since 1962. As I talked long distance to other fellows from the team, it was clear that no one knew where Tom was or what he was doing. Tom was the lone mystery player.

Just prior to the reunion, my telephone rang, and to my utter amazement, Tom was on the line calling from a city hundreds of miles away. He had no knowledge of the reunion; he had had no contact with anyone from the past team. He had just felt the sudden urge, after nineteen years, to look me up, and he spontaneously followed through. We had a catch-up conversation, at the end of which he accepted my invitation to the reunion.

How did that happen? What forces were set in motion to create that result? Was it coincidence or serendipity, or was something more powerful, beyond human consciousness, at work? You decide.

My second example is one that happened in 2007. My wife and I were walking back to our home in La Quinta, California, from the exercise facility at the PGA West golf club. One of the topics that came up as we walked and talked was where we wanted to live. Although we both loved our house, we envisioned expanding what we already had. We had a detailed and lively dialogue about what our dream home would look like—more space, a view of the fairways and the mountains, private offices, no golf cart path out front, a quieter neighborhood overlooking the numerous lakes that dot the course, larger patios, more spacious living quarters, and a few other conveniences and amenities.

At one point my wife casually looked to her left and said, "Something similar to that one."

I turned to see what she was referring to, and there it was. From the exterior it was an identical match regarding what we had just brainstormed. A realtor's sign hung from a white post stuck in the manicured front lawn, but the sign said "Sold."

Darn, I thought, but I wasn't ready to make a move at that time anyway. We were just having a discussion—or so I thought. We could see that the front door was slightly ajar, and out of curiosity, we decided to investigate. A grumpy, slightly disheveled older man answered the door and asked us what we wanted. We exchanged introductions and learned that he was the real estate agent who had negotiated the sale of the property.

Somewhat aggressively I said, "We're curious what the property sold for and whether you know of any other similar homes that might be available in the immediate area."

He paused, shaking his head from side to side, looked down at the ground, and replied, "Come on in. This is a long, sad story. I'm frustrated about this so-called deal." As we stood in the kitchen, casually casing the place, he continued.

"This place has been in escrow for almost a year and the buyer can't, or won't, remove the one remaining deal-killing contingency. The seller is a friend of mine, an elderly widow who lives out of town, and she doesn't seem to care. She doesn't need the money, but my commission has been held up for too long. I'm not in this business to be a custodian and property manager. I want this deal closed and over with."

Hmmm, I thought, *here's an opportunity, perhaps.*

We continued the conversation as we took a brief tour of the house, then we sat around the dining room table. The house was just what my wife and I had described moments earlier, especially with its incredible view of the mountains and the lake just beyond the tiled patio.

"I don't know all of the legalities of real estate law in California," I said, "but if I made you an offer, signed a purchase agreement, and left you a check right now for the down payment, would you see if you could force the deal and legally eliminate the current buyer? Or, at the very least, force a decision?"

"Are you serious?"

Before I could respond, my wife replied, "Yes, we're very serious."

The Universe had apparently been eavesdropping during our conversation and was opening doors, literally. The momentum increased and accelerated rapidly to action.

The end result after many phone calls and papers signed in bankers' and lawyers' offices was that we moved in six weeks later, having sold our house to the first interested buyer. Sometimes the Universe responds quickly and you had better be prepared to act. If you don't, the opportunity fades away. Opportunities eventually quit knocking.

"At times we shall simply have to admit that, one way or another,
what we can neither explain nor understand certainly doesn't
cease to exist because we cannot see how it does or why it should."
—Dr. Mark Hyman, author, The Five Forces of Wellness

Life can be, and remains to me, an enticing mystery, as Dr. Mark Hyman suggests. Be open to the unexplained possibilities in your own life. Be open to the possibility that science, basic psychology, and what are referred to as spiritual or metaphysical universal laws are not necessarily in opposition to one another. There is much in the Universe that we cannot prove unequivocally. The best we can do is to stay open, explore, and make our own conclusions based on our individual experiences of life. You must decide what is valid and what will work for you. Remember, you will filter your conclusions through your conditioned core beliefs, and what you believe to be true will influence and determine your reality.

What you focus on expands and attracts to you the corresponding vibration or frequency match in the Universe. Quantum physics suggests that experimenters and scientists can influence the result of an experiment by their thoughts, expectations, and intentions regarding the outcome. This is known among scientists as the "experimenter expectancy effect." There is scientific support for that premise. The Law of Attraction is similar to the quantum realm in outcomes.

Thoughts are believed to be energy and will seek, attract, and influence similar energy fields that saturate and circumvent the Universe. You can and will sway the end result.

If my primary consciousness is about abundance and prosperity, I will attract similar vibration fields of abundance and prosperity to myself as long as my core beliefs support the outcome and I am not attempting to con myself. The rich do get richer. Like attracts like—not opposites, as is popularly believed and preached by many as an exact truth. If my primary consciousness is about what I lack and about poverty, I will attract that to me. The poor who focus on their poverty do get poorer.

Google "Law of Attraction," examine the voluminous research, opinions, current facts, and fiction, and decide for yourself. Let me repeat a word of caution one more time: The more entrenched you are in your inflexible position, the less open you will be to the possibilities offered by the Universe and by sources outside of your discipline and conditioned core beliefs.

The Law of Attraction receives a substantial boost once your core beliefs, vision, goals, and affirmations are in place and in alignment with internal mechanisms—what Dr. Maltz referred to as early as 1960 as your psycho-cybernetics. The Universe is in partnership with basic psychology and normal functions of the brain. I want to discuss three of the partnering mechanisms that propel you to achieve what you want more of: the reticular activation system, cognitive dissonance, and the teleological nature of human beings.

The Reticular Activating System

Located at the core of the brainstem and sandwiched between the medulla oblongata and the midbrain is the reticular activating system (RAS). This pinkie-size network of cells is the center for arousal and motivation, and it contributes substantially to maintaining a high state of consciousness. It also serves as a central clearinghouse, filing, scrutinizing, and censoring incoming data regarding what is relevant and important to you.

The RAS provides a discriminating filter that allows into your awareness critical data that heighten your sense of urgency, look out for your safety, reinforce your beliefs, and shine light upon the path to your specific goals.

Without the RAS, each of us would be overwhelmed by the massive volume of unsolicited stimuli that assaults our consciousness. We would be made aware of every sensation in our bodies, such as feeling every hair move on our skin or hearing every noise in the background. We would be distracted by sidebar conversations and the avalanche of headline news, radio broadcasts, and myriad other enticements that spontaneously come our way. The RAS is like an internal receptionist or discriminating administrative assistant who is dedicated to letting in only those calls and appointments that are consistent with our interests, thus providing for our sanity and ability to stay focused.

When you set a goal, and when you affirm, picture, and emote feelings relative to that desired outcome, the RAS is activated, and it goes to work selecting data that will propel you toward your goal. Your awareness is now open and receptive to what it is you need to do in order to complete the goal and actualize the affirmation.

If, for example, you have an interest in attending one of Dr. Wayne Dyer's self-actualization seminars, your awareness opens and is directed by the RAS as it sorts and discovers data that will accelerate your meeting that goal. For the first time, you notice consciously and take interest in the direct mail advertisement sent out by Dr. Dyer's sponsors that comes across your desk. You discover books written by Dr. Dyer as you casually browse the shelves at the airport kiosk in between flights. The book titles seem to be magnified in bold print, and they seem to literally tumble off the shelves and into your hands. Suddenly you overhear strangers talking about how great the Dyer workshops are. You surf TV channels one evening and notice that PBS is broadcasting a seminar by Dr. Dyer at seven o'clock. And the beat goes on. All of those data were previously out there for your scrutiny, but they had been filtered out of your awareness. There was no sense of urgency, nor did you have a desire or need to absorb, experience, or review that information. With your interest awakened, your RAS magnet can now zero in on and attract to you—and you to it—all that you need to know about attending Dr. Dyer's seminars.

People are often baffled when a path, such as this example illustrates, starts to unfold unexpectedly. They credit blind luck, serendipity, or being at the right place at the right time. Some call it riding the wave of the zone or going with the flow. From a mechanistic, cybernetic standpoint, what they are experiencing is an internal capability that most healthy and normal functioning human beings share. It is their RAS operating by design. From the viewpoint of the Universe, the Law of Attraction is assisting people by matching up similar frequencies and vibrations. A joint venture is being formed by bringing together internal and external forces.

No matter what you believe is the actual cause, the effect remains the same. Do not get hung up on being right or righteous about the source. You are being shown explicitly the path and the data needed to reach the goal. Act upon the path and data, and more will follow as the momentum toward the desired outcome accelerates. Ignore them, and the information will remain in your blind spot, or you will dismiss it altogether and move on. All is not lost, however; additional help is on the way through a psychological phenomenon called cognitive dissonance. Here is how it works.

Cognitive Dissonance

Cognitive dissonance is a psychological state that aids us in resolving and diminishing the feelings of tension and anxiety we suffer when two opposing thoughts simultaneously occupy or influence our minds. It exists when there is incompatibility among the thoughts, the core beliefs, and the transformation or change we desire and are moving toward.

For example, you might set a goal of becoming well organized. You are affirming and picturing that outcome and thus feeling great about yourself and your goal. Your current reality, however, reflects that you are still a bit messy and disorganized. The disparity between what you are experiencing presently and what you want to experience in the near future creates the dissonance that results in anxiety, tension, and confusion. This state of cognitive dissonance can assist you in changing the no longer desired behavior of being disorganized. By focusing on the desired new behavior, you can control the disorganization, put it to rest forever, and reach your goal of being organized. But you must move toward the goal with intentional focus, affirmations, mental pictures, and accompanying emotions that propel you toward a different outcome. If you meekly attempt to change while doing what you have always been doing, you'll experience the same or similar negative emotions as you did before.

The automatic engaging of cognitive dissonance will resolve your situation according to the degree of intensity you assign to each of the following issues:

- How important the resolved outcome(s) might be to you

- How wide the disparity is among your thoughts, beliefs, circumstances, and the desired new outcome(s)

- How difficult it is to justify or rationalize the disparity

- How much the conflict magnifies or opposes your core beliefs or your experience of yourself (this means you are an observer of your life and aware of yourself)
- How committed you are to experience the new outcome(s)

The structural tension and anxiety between what is true about your situation (a messy and disorganized life) and the desired outcome (a well-organized and newly ordered life) will trigger creative and innovative actions and behaviors that, with focus and attention, move you toward being better organized. The Law of Attraction is engaged and brings to you organization protocols and systems, news of organizational seminars and workshops, and experts and publications on the topic that will assist and guide you. The RAS comes into play in this focused process and directs the information that you need into your consciousness, which further leads and directs you to the end result you desire.

The disparity between what you have and what you want forces the cognitive mind to scan for, obtain, create, initiate, and invent new ways of framing and thinking about the situation, thereby eliminating, or substantially diminishing, the dissonance. The mind is compelled to resolve the dissonance. Ideas and actions will follow to push you toward being more organized.

It is essential that you focus totally on the new objective with passion and that you give minimum time or energy to the past—except to notice and record the progress you are making as you move toward what you are attempting to change. Again, it is the union between the Universe and what is considered in the field of the behavioral sciences as sound psychology that propels you to what you really want and deserve in life. It is all about experiencing your desires, living the existence that you choose to live from a balanced platform, and getting on with your life and all that is available to you.

The Teleological Nature of Human Beings

The teleological nature of "normal, functioning" human beings is defined among numerous philosophical and psychological interpretations as reaching a concluding end having been driven by a directed purpose and cause. We are formed and shaped by our ambitions, passions, core beliefs, dreams, and images—all of which we've adapted and adjusted along the way to meet the picture of our imagined new and exciting status.

In multiple ways, you are quite similar to a powered guided missile or rocket that, as it's heading for a distant target, is off course by either wide or narrow degrees most of the journey. Technology and mechanisms inside the "mind/computer" of the rocket make careful and immediate complicated calculations to keep the rocket on target, adjusting for gravitational pull, imbalance in the propulsion system, human error, asteroids in the path, or whatever else might influence the rocket to head in the wrong direction. The teleological mechanisms inside of you, similar in function to the state-of-the-art digital technology inside the rocket, keep you moving toward your goals, adjusting and self-correcting consciously and unconsciously along the way to the desired outcome. These mechanisms provide you with the energy, time management skills, and correct decisions necessary for you to reach your desired focused goal.

Lou Tice, founder of the Pacific Institute, says, "Remember to seek feedback and make adjustments. You are teleological in nature. A teleological mechanism can change directions after it's released. It doesn't care where it starts; it only cares where it is now in relation to where it intends to be. As you expand where you belong, you allow yourself to move in the direction without negative feedback causing you to go back to 'where you belong.'"

Have you ever noticed that when you feel pushed and pulled positively toward an end result that you are passionate about and focused on, time and energy take on new dimensions? The best way I can personally describe this phenomenon is that I no longer have a reasonable relationship with either time or energy. Hours can pass and I hardly notice their passage. My energy seems boundless even though I have not eaten for hours. These experiences occur when I write a manuscript or design a new training module. I am somehow drawn relentlessly to the activity with joy and increased infatuation. And course corrections are being made automatically, with minimal conscious thought, forced maneuvering, or detailed analysis.

You have your own version of such experiences. You know what it's like to become focused totally in an activity that you are passionate about and devoted to. Maybe it is building furniture in your garage workshop with your inventory of specialized tools. Perhaps it is weeding and planting flowers in your luscious, undisciplined English garden; spending intimate time with a loved one; or acting in a local amateur production of a classic Broadway play. The experience seems spiritual in nature as you are in the flow, experiencing yourself at a higher level. Or the experience is simply our inherent teleological state in motion and being actualized. It possibly could be both.

You are on a journey to an end result that is shaped and crafted by your imagination and creative powers. The old rules are cast away in favor of the miraculous tools and capabilities that lie within you. I believe that this circumstance is our natural spiritual existence, but we have been conditioned by external influences—schools, governments, religions, educational institutions, families, and the military, among others—to believe it is neither a natural process nor our inherent ability.

An abundance of tools and mechanisms are available to you to transform your hopes and dreams into reality. The sources and inventory seem to be unlimited and at your fingertips. Do not limit your potential and possibilities by core belief systems that are narrow, rigid, prejudicial, and restrictive. What you have may pale in comparison with what you might create and experience in the future. Let the Universe and sound psychology work out the details. Your role is to set the partnership in motion by your willful acknowledgment that these forces are your advocates. Seemingly mutually exclusive of one another, they can nevertheless set in motion the life that really matters to you.

EXERCISES

- What circumstances in your life prevent you from living in the "now"? How much time do you spend living in the past or worrying about the future? How can you refocus and be in the present?

- What is on your daily to-do list that you can eliminate or hand off to others? Prioritize your list and reduce the number of items to the five most important that are essential to you. Make this list the evening before the next day's activities.

- What moment or event in your life has been the one that has most defined you? Is it positive or negative? If it's negative, how can you reinvent yourself and recast your story with a more positive outcome?

- Reflect on your past and identify a positive event that you cannot rationally understand or explain. What happened? What did you set in motion to create this occurrence? What was the objective? What thoughts were you thinking? What were you envisioning? Where was your energy level? How did you experience the passage of time?

CHAPTER 3
A ROAD TO MORE

The highest manifestation of life consists in this: that a being
governs its own actions. A thing which is always subject to
the direction of another is somewhat of a dead thing.

—SAINT THOMAS AQUINAS
ITALIAN PHILOSOPHER AND THEOLOGIAN

There are multiple ways to achieve what you say you want more of.
This creation process is what many other successful people have
undertaken to manifest a life that is meaningful to them. In this
chapter I will introduce you to the fundamentals you will need to
work from to begin getting more out of your life. Whether you decide
to tweak the methodology to fit your personality or style of thinking,
or you accept it as is, your active participation is required. You cannot download this software in a plug-and-play model. As comedian
George Carlin quipped, "I went to a bookstore and asked the sales-
woman, 'Where's the self-help section?' She said if she told me, it

would defeat the purpose." Getting more of what you aspire to have in life and the manner in which you go about it is ultimately up to you.

EXPAND YOUR AWARENESS

Do what you need to do to improve and expand your awareness. Support and focus teams, mentors, coaches, advisers, and mastermind groups are helpful. I recommend that you choose your supporting cast and select wisely. Surround yourself with people who have been where you want to go. They know the road and have the maps. It is comforting to have trusted people who have a sincere interest in your success to run ideas by and receive sound advice from. Seek out people who will tell you the truth as they see it. Remain open to feedback so you can correct your course if you are wavering.

As you become more successful, you will automatically attract people with whom you have more in common and who can guide you further along your path. Those you attract are familiar with these time-tested techniques and can tap into a natural internal process of manifestation. Everything that you desire, within reason, is available to you when you are fully aligned with the Universe. Remember, when I use the word "Universe," I am referring to an entity defined by you that assists you in having more of what you aspire to. It is what you consider to be your higher power. If you do not already have what you aspire to, but have declared it, know that it is on its way. Be patient.

Beyond Limitations

A clear-cut example of going beyond limitations is the story of Team Hoyt, told in their book, *It's Only a Mountain: Dick and Rick Hoyt, Men of Iron.* This memoir shows how the father-son team saw possibilities and created inexplicable results that reached far beyond reasonable expectations.

I first learned of Team Hoyt while watching *Wide World of Sports* in 1988. ABC televised the Ironman World Triathlon Championship from Hawaii Island. The team set an example for others to emulate. I watched and cheered for twenty-eight-year-old Ricky, afflicted with cerebral palsy and a quadriplegic since birth, compete with his forty-eight-year-old father, Dick, in the most grueling athletic event on the planet. They are a devoted and awesome "anything's possible" team.

They competed fiercely, without self-imposed limitations, but did not win the event. They did win the hearts and minds of many who observed their incredible effort, including mine. Seeing what Ricky and Dick were able to accomplish, I realized there was no more room in my life for reasons, excuses, or rationalizations. From that point on, I could be a writer; I could be a keynote speaker; I could be in a loving, intimate relationship; I could have prosperity; and I could inspire, influence, and transform others. I could! I had no doubt. There was no looking back. If the Hoyts could do what I watched them do, I could reach my dreams. So can you. Be inspired and transfer your inspiration and dreams into tangible and visible action.

My limitations were less severe than were Ricky's. It's humbling. When I entered the public school system in Tacoma, Washington, I was separated immediately from my new classmates; I was examined, poked, probed, and tested by experts with, by today's standards, primitive equipment and processes. I was diagnosed as being somewhat slow. After further testing and observation, "somewhat slow" was reclassified and upgraded by the examiners to "intelligent," but my significant speech impediment remained, which required the attention of Tacoma School District speech therapists. I had difficulty enunciating words. I mixed up syllables, often putting them in incongruent order or accenting the wrong one when reading aloud. As a result, my strategy was to speak rapidly to get the reading over with as quickly as possible, which compounded the problem. I slurred words and jammed sentences together so that my speech was almost incomprehensible to my teachers and classmates.

It was embarrassing to be singled out, publicly corrected, excused from group-reading exercises, and sent off to remedial reading sessions with other students who were labeled handicapped. I began forming a belief about myself that I would trip over for years to come.

Frustrated by having an identified speaking impediment, I simply did not say anything, hardly responding to questions or contributing to the simplest discussions. Silence became my self-determined defense. Being dumb provided me with an escape hatch, a sanctuary away from the scrutiny and labels of the experts and the unmerciful teasing of my classmates. Consequently, I was also classified as being overly shy. I began to shut down and pull inside myself. I became a turtle. It was the safest strategy I could come up with at the time under those conditions. The labels were beginning to define me, and they were gaining momentum and substance. My self-concept and core beliefs about myself continued to take form.

None of those behaviors, experiences, core beliefs, and impairments qualified or prepared me to become a world-class international keynote speaker. But I am. Look at my website, www.influencemany. com, and decide for yourself. People who knew me from the distant past and in my teenage years are astonished to discover that I am a successful keynote speaker. "Ole Carlson is an international keynote speaker? Are you kidding me? Good for him," I often hear whispered behind my back. It makes me smile.

I believe my humble journey is the exception and not the prevailing rule. It took considerable study, effort, vision, courage, determination, focus, and passion on my part to shed all of the shame, labels, limitations, mistakes, and past embarrassments. But I did—and so can you. I am proud, joyful, and grateful for what I have accomplished. What do you want to accomplish?

What I achieved may not be on the same scale as others' achievements, but it was monumental to me, as your achievements will be to you. You have your own relative situation in some aspect of your life. I wish you even more success than I have enjoyed. Perhaps you will accomplish it faster and with more ease, with fewer obstacles to overcome.

Marshall Faulk, whose inspiring foreword you read when you opened *Aspire*, says

Is it hard? It's hard. I mean, it's not easy. There's some work that's involved. But it's just like everything else—you work for it, you get it . . . There are kids at home scratching their heads like, "Oh, boy. I don't have what it takes to make it because I can't run the football like he does." That has nothing to do with it. When I talk to kids, I let them know it's not about that. You can do it. You don't have to be a football player to do it.

You can do whatever your "it" is, within reason. You can change careers at almost any point in your life. You can become a doctor, lawyer, teacher, or whatever your passion drives you toward. Make the commitment. Figure out what it is that you have to do to get what you aspire to. Then either do it or settle for what you have. Remember what I said in chapter 1: At the end of any given day, you have either created value or waste. You get to choose between status quo or remarkable, familiar or extraordinary, comfortable or being stretched to the borders and beyond. It is your choice.

KEEP IT REAL

I want people to succeed, not to be positioned for failure because of false or completely unrealistic expectations—their own or those of others. As you learned in the previous chapter, certain principles and natural laws of the Universe will assist you in your journey to your potential. I believe in the Law of Attraction. I believe that like attracts like, that we draw to us those things that we think most about, and that what we focus on expands. I believe that all thoughts are energy that reaches out to an expansive and giving Universe.

I further believe that the mechanism—namely, you and I—that is attracting the desired outcome must be fully functional and capable of transmitting the correct frequency and coordinates to the Universe with good intent. If the vibration is weak, ill intended, ego based, and confused, the result will be less than anticipated, and certainly less than is necessary to achieve or sustain the desired outcome. All cylinders must be firing, and you must be willing and able to do the work required.

The issue is not about limitations—self-imposed or innate. It is more about how you can adjust your intentions, desires, core beliefs, values, and actions to be in alignment with what is available to you in the Universe. The possibilities are limitless. Your connection with the Universe will expand what is possible for you and propel you to your outer boundaries. The radar works perfectly; the operator is usually the one in error.

What follows is a simple comparison of people who realize a large percentage of their potential and those who realize a small percentage. Those in the first category have designed for themselves a remarkable life of high achievement; those in the second category have resigned themselves to live an unremarkable life of low achievement.

A high achiever is someone who succeeds in doing, usually through focused effort. High achievers choose to attain, get, realize, and accomplish. Low achievers choose to fail.

Someone who lives a remarkable life attracts attention because they are unusual or exceptional, and they are worth noticing and commenting on. They have chosen to be extraordinary, amazing, notable, and noteworthy. Someone who lives an unremarkable life has chosen to be ordinary.

The Haves **People who experience a large percentage of their potential**	**The Have-nots** **People who experience a small percentage of their potential**
Choose **accountability** for all of their results, both good and bad	Choose **subordination** and become victims and martyrs
Choose **clarity** as a strategy and create what they desire	Choose **confusion** as a strategy and remain stuck
Consistently use **positive self-talk**	Consistently use **negative self-talk**
Focus on the **positive pictures** of their lives	Focus on the **negative pictures** of their lives
Consistently feel **positive emotions**	Consistently feel **negative emotions**
Remain **real**	Remain in **denial**

If you find yourself in the right-hand column, yet you have passion and desire and are motivated to overcome obstacles to migrate to the left-hand column, this book will provide you with the tools, techniques, and knowledge to make the journey. The left-hand column is the consistent and predictable domain of high performers and the template that we will explore throughout the rest of the book to help you create a remarkable life. This is the manifestation process of high achievers and successful, self-actualized people. If you are secure in the left-hand column and wonder how you got there, now you know. With that knowledge, you can intentionally replicate the process to expand your life even further in areas where you aspire to grow. You can teach others how to get to where you are and enjoy what the Universe has to offer. That is what true leadership and self-actualization are all about.

If you find yourself in the right-hand column, lacking motivation and/or the desire to consciously journey to the left, you do not get to complain because it is your choice. If you have come up light in the gene pool, do the best you can nonetheless with what you have, and see how far you can move the needle toward remarkable. For others of you, it could be that the time is not right; you are simply worn out. Rest yourself, then take small steps toward becoming a high achiever. For others still, the obstacle may be obscure, or it is too painful to identify. You may just be one of those people who settle and accept their self-inflicted fate.

The tools, techniques, and knowledge that I offer in this book will do you no good unless you are committed to be accountable and willing to implement the process. My wish for you is that you are able to make that choice. The Universe is poised and waiting for you to engage in a positive and constructive manner. It just takes a little success to fuel the rest of the journey, but you have to start. Are you ready?

SUBORDINATION OR ACCOUNTABILITY?

In order to get the most out of your life, you need to decide who is standing at the front of the room. Get up there! This is the launching pad where creating a remarkable life gets significant acceleration and liftoff. It is your individual call. If you are unwilling to accept that you are in charge and that you are accountable for your results—good and bad—there is no reason for you to continue on this journey. This is not an ego-based stance. You must own responsibility to move forward.

You are just wasting time if aspiring is all about your ego wanting to satisfy your insatiable thirst for attention or for more tangible goods. If this describes what drives you, get used to where you are and what you have. Tomorrow is going to be a replica of what you experienced today. It is going to be the same old same old.

Here are your fundamental choices: You can create a life of *resignation* (subordination) or a life of *designation* (accountability). That's it. There are no manifestation secrets behind door number three because there is no third door. Subordination and accountability are the two options available to you, and the results for each path are significantly different. Remember my motto: Each day you get to create value or waste. Which way of life do you want to choose?

If you choose a life of *resignation*, the locus of control is external. You show up, become subordinate, and receive whatever comes your way, good or bad. You will become the clown at the rear of the parade with the wheelbarrow, shovel, and broom, sweeping and scooping up the droppings of life. But you do not get to whine about that result if it is not exactly what you had in mind. Your outcomes will be consistent and predictable, and in the end, disappointing. If you do feel the need for a dramatic hissy fit, go ahead and throw a pity party. But you will attract and create only more of whatever you are whining about. Welcome to the world of victims, martyrs, and people who are stuck in life and locked into their assigned roles. Decide that you deserve better and take action.

If you choose a life of true *designation*, the locus of control is internal. You show up, initiate ideas, take appropriate action, and receive what you wanted more of with joy and gratitude. You are the leader of the great marching band at the head of the Fourth of July parade, creating the excitement. It is a preview of what is to follow as you strut down the parade route. And you get to take credit for it, along with your loving and faithful, ever-imaginative cocreator, the Universe.

Hear the music, feel the excitement of the crowd, watch the clock ticking away the seconds! Is it going to be door number one or door number two? Bandleader out in front, or clown in the rear? It's your life, your future, your choice.

CONFUSION OR CLARITY?

Get a clear vision. Otherwise, you may wander to unproductive areas that do not serve you or others. *Clarity* means "to be accurate of thought, reasoning, and expression; to have freedom from indistinctness or ambiguity." Your next step is to take time to explore and decide on what you want more of, what you aspire to blissfully.

Hear your voice—not the needs and wants of others. Those voices come and go. Yours is with you for the entire start-to-finish ride. The outcomes that others suggest for you might be similar to yours, but until you declare what you want, you will be living a life for others. You will remain out of alignment with your purpose, vision, values, and spirit. Do you recall Maria Shriver's pledge to ask herself "Who am I? What do I believe in? What am I grateful for? What do I want my life to stand for?"

Unless you are certain about what you aspire to, life has this irritating and arrogant habit of whisking you away from your goals whenever and wherever it decides. Life does not offer many transfer slips, rain checks, or meal vouchers. High-achievers invest considerable time, energy, focus, and conscious, intentional thought at this formulation stage of the manifestation process. They invest heavily in determining what they want more of because they know that the remaining steps subsequently fall into sequence once aspirations are secured with proper and appropriate intention.

Nothing is created without a preceding thought. Perhaps the thought is to be still and let creativity run its course, allowing new ideas into your consciousness. If you remain aware, you have the opportunity to create and control your thoughts, one conscious thought at a time. You eliminate the helter-skelter chaos and panic that permeate many people's lives. You give yourself the option of moving forward and not allocating your life to chance, or to the absolute control and external input of others.

A crystal clear idea of what you want in your life is the fuel that helps you stay conscious and switch from unaware autopilot to manual hands-on control. Grab the control stick once you have clarity. You can let go and enjoy the ride once the process has momentum and is firing on all cylinders, the destination coordinates are in place, and the runway is cleared.

If you are more invested in the how—the process—instead of the what—the outcome—you have it backward. Trust that along with clarity of what you aspire to comes the how. If having all your ducks lined up is more essential than figuring out and declaring where you want to go, you will be preoccupied and obsessed with arranging useless logistics instead of enjoying the fruits of the yet-to-be-determined destination. You will wind up somewhere, but it may not be where you had in mind.

I am not suggesting that you be completely reckless in your planning and calculating. I am suggesting that once you get clear about your goals, the path to what you want more of will appear and self-correct automatically. The Universe and the self-correcting mechanisms of the subconscious will provide you with the road map and the compass. Napoleon Hill in *Think and Grow Rich* states, "Our brains become magnetized with the dominating thoughts which we hold in our minds, and, by means with which no man is familiar, these 'magnets' attract to us the forces, the people, the circumstances of life which harmonize with the nature of our dominating thoughts."

This is the opposite of conservation fishing, which is enforced when there is a limited supply of fish. In conservation fishing, you catch and release. You, however, will release and catch. The more willing you are to release—to remove yourself from the need to control the process—the easier it will be to fill your creel. You can have whatever it is you are attempting to catch. You get to keep it without having to worry that it will evaporate whenever your guard is down.

The alternative strategy in life is to remain confused and overwhelmed with the choices that confront you, allowing paralysis to eventually set in. You end up procrastinating about making important decisions and postponing life-enhancing goals. You scratch your head and ask yourself repeatedly, "Should I or shouldn't I? Will it work out or not? Is this the right time, or should I wait? What will people think? What's holding me back? What should I do? Is there somebody who can tell me what to do next?" The rug beneath your feet becomes worn thin as you pace back and forth questioning your next move. The questions become irritating, confusing, and frustrating when you implement—consciously or unconsciously—a stagnant strategy to freeze-dry your life.

The more confused you are, the greater the number of confusing thoughts you attract. They pour into your consciousness, crowding out productive, problem-solving considerations. The more questions you ask yourself, the more questions you create. The questions spread like a software virus in a computer hard drive, permeating your every thought. Your hard drive is now corrupted and you shut down.

This relentless self-interrogation holds rescuing answers in abeyance, circling in formation like stacked airplanes hovering above an overcrowded, overbooked, O'Hare Airport in the midst of thunderstorms. You have clogged up the landing zone with confusion and clutter.

Other analogies come to mind that may help you get the picture. The faucet is now turned on full force and you cannot turn it off. Or you keep hearing a song over and over in your head, and it's the very song you do not—I repeat, you do not—want to hear any longer. Or you've become the poster child for a deer in the headlights. Paralysis sets in. The sun sinks below the horizon on another day during which you made little movement toward creating the life that you really desire. A new day dawns, but only because of repetition can it limp along.

We discussed in chapter 1 some of the roadblocks that inhibit you from gaining clarity and declaring what is important to you. Review that section and decide which specific roadblock is preventing you from accelerating toward what you really desire in your life. What is holding you back? It is time to be honest beyond reproach.

DENIAL OR BEING REAL?

In order to move forward, it is essential that you be honest with yourself and open yourself to an awareness of what could be instead of what is. Author Simon Travaglia believes that "the greatest barrier to someone achieving their potential is their denial of it." What do you believe to be true about yourself and the power of your Universe—your potential? Are you seeing yourself and the situation that you are in through subjective or objective eyes? The pathway to sustained growth is to be curious, available, and open to other possibilities. How open are you to learning what you don't know and the possibilities beyond?

To what extent is filtering or erroneous thinking blocking you from accessing the potential that you and the Universe possess and thus preventing you from experiencing what brings you total fulfillment?

Where in your life do you continue to set goals with seemingly good intentions and using proper mechanics, yet you find yourself consistently coming just shy of the desired outcome? Are you seeing the obstacles as they are rather than how you have been conditioned to view them? Are you setting the bar too low or too high because you are unwilling to do the work? Where do you settle for less because the beliefs needed to succeed elude you or you refuse to acknowledge that those beliefs might be valid?

The denial and realism pendulum swings both ways. You can be in denial about the possibilities in your life, your open-ended potential—what you see through your windshield. You can also be in denial about what is holding you back, the obstacles to your happiness and success—what you see in your rearview mirror.

English social reformer and theosophist Annie Besant once wrote, "Refusal to believe until proof is given is a rational position; denial of all outside of our own limited experience is absurd." Bouncing back and forth somewhere between rational thinking and absurdity is the place that might work for you. You may have no idea how much fun pushing against the borders of absurdity is, within reason.

It would be undoubtedly absurd and outright irresponsible to believe that you could fly like a bird without any mechanical assistance and expert training. That is what I deem unreasonable. To nosedive off a high cliff, jagged rocks waiting menacingly below, with only positive thinking, mental pictures, emotions, and faith providing the lift beneath your spread-eagle, featherless arms, would be stupid and irrational. You would be in denial about the ultimate consequences, or simply trying to commit suicide.

It would be more rational to believe that, after proper research and instruction, one could figure out a way to soar birdlike into rising wind currents using a device such as a hang glider or parasail.

This approach would be driven more by practical realism, and the end result would be more predictable.

I use the example of flying because some people, after attending one of my seminars, have challenged me, asserting, "Carlson, if what you say is true, certainly anything in life is within our reach. If these tenets are valid, then they should apply everywhere under all conditions, and we should be able to affirm ourselves into flying like a bird." The challenge is valid from the participant's point of view, but the absurdity of the premise illustrates the denial of the person and their unwillingness to learn as they continue to defend what they know.

Be somewhat reasonable with yourself, especially if this material is new. Use your open-ended-possibilities brain and not your doubts and judgments. I want you to experience success, not frustration. As you begin to experience more of what is possible for you, then you can become more aggressive and start to stretch to your outer limits. Forget the unaided plunge off the cliff. That's lunacy, and it will prevent you from finishing this book.

Being logical, sensible, practical, realistic, and evenhanded will be replaced gradually with guiding principles of being a bit illogical, somewhat irrational and impractical, and viewing your world and life from previously unrealistic vantage points. What might have seemed unrealistic may draw within your grasp in the future. Your journey awaits you.

EXERCISES

- In what areas of your life do you take full accountability for creating? What areas do you not? What are the differences?

- Where in your life do you remain confused about the next step? Where are you crystal clear about the next step?

- Describe your self-talk when you do not meet your standards. Describe your self-talk when you meet or exceed your expectations.

- Fast-forward five years and describe the success and happiness you see yourself enjoying. What are you saying to yourself about your achievements? How does that feel?

- Do you sincerely believe that you can reach the milestones that you set for yourself? If not, what are your obstacles?

CHAPTER 4

CONDITIONING THE INNOCENT

Believe nothing just because a so-called wise person said it.
Believe nothing just because a belief is generally held.
Believe nothing just because it is said in ancient books.
Believe nothing just because it is said to be of divine origin.
Believe nothing just because someone else believes it.
Believe what you yourself test and judge to be true.

**—SIDDHARTHA GAUTAMA
INDIAN PHILOSOPHER AND FOUNDER OF BUDDHISM**

The manifestation process requires you to examine your core beliefs
and past conditioning and to identify your basic assumptions about
life. Most of your beliefs were absorbed unconsciously before the age
of ten. These core beliefs and assumptions will be the foundation and
launching pad for what is to follow as you continue your journey.
They will either propel you ahead to what you aspire to have more of,
or they will limit what is possible.

Your mission, values, and goals will be deeply rooted and aligned with what you believe to be true. Just because you have believed something for a long time doesn't necessarily make it true, nor does it automatically make it worthy enough to be passed on to others. Long-term belief in something doesn't mean that that something will contribute to your life positively. Let's challenge the traditional and self-limiting sound bites that permeate our lives and corral our futures, and force them to march in lockstep. What follows is a list of some of the thoughtless pearls of wisdom that can limit your thinking:

- Follow the rules.
- Be politically correct.
- Stay the course.
- All good things must come to an end.
- The odds are against you.
- Opposites attract.
- The early bird gets the worm.
- Don't judge a book by its cover.
- Don't look a gift horse in the mouth.
- All things in moderation.
- The squeaky wheel gets the grease.
- Silence is golden.
- The truth will set you free.
- Ignorance is bliss.
- Bide your time.
- Turn the other cheek.
- Too many cooks will spoil the broth.

- Life is difficult; then you die.
- This is the way we've always done it.
- That's just the way it is.
- A good man/woman is hard to find.
- Stay between the lines.

Challenge these and the myriad other inside-the-box, mindless messages that promote self-limiting core beliefs. Many of these "jewels" create predictable, familiar, comfortable, and no-growth results. Lives spent following these platitudes end, all too quickly it seems, with the individuals' potential going with them to the grave.

Some methodologies in the manifestation process work better than others. These options are the ones that are in more secure alignment with the natural laws of the Universe and the creative process. For instance, you can clench your fists, grit your teeth, and grind your way to the end. That works—it's the American way. You can luck out and win the lottery. Good luck is a gift; accept it. You can outsmart your way to the end, beat the odds, or be in the right spot at the right time. You can control and micromanage all external elements of your life and get what you aspire to, but you risk being too exhausted to enjoy it.

You can also get clear about what you believe to be true, aspire to what you really want in life, watch the results those beliefs are creating, and be willing to take a different path if the outcomes are not satisfying. Nelson Mandela, anti-apartheid activist and former president of South Africa, believes that "One of the most difficult things is not to change society, but to change yourself." Start with upping the ante on your personal transformation. Don't simply pursue incremental, play-it-safe, change-the-world strategies. Don't fix your focus upon others to avoid what *you* need to do to become better.

Minor League baseball catcher Crash Davis in the movie *Bull Durham* was gin clear on what he believed in. When Annie Savoy, perpetual predator of the Durham Bulls' rookies, asked him what he believed in, Crash answered without hesitation:

> Well, I believe in the soul . . . the small of a woman's back, the hanging curve ball, high fiber, good scotch, that the novels of Susan Sontag are self-indulgent, overrated crap. I believe Lee Harvey Oswald acted alone. I believe there ought to be a constitutional amendment outlawing Astroturf and the designated hitter. I believe in the sweet spot, soft-core pornography, opening your presents Christmas morning rather than Christmas Eve, and I believe in long, slow, deep, soft, wet kisses that last three days.

Not all of those beliefs and assumptions served Crash to any great extent, nor did he leave a notable legacy in his wake. They did not make his life more noble or the world a better place. But you must admit, he had clarity extraordinaire. The quotation illustrates how people can have top-of-mind awareness of their position in life and what they believe to be true. I'm not certain that I could rattle off my beliefs and assumptions in that many aspects of my life at such a rapid pace. Could you?

FLOURISH FACTORS

While living in Seattle and facilitating Vistage CEO groups, I brought in transformational speaker and executive coach Nikki Nemerouf to speak to my team of sixteen highly successful local CEOs whose companies had from $5 million to $1 billion in annual sales. Nikki identified four factors that help leaders flourish.

- Triggered-state recovery: the ability to make a rapid shift from a flight-fight-freeze-appease state to one of cognitive thinking when you perceive that there is a real, imagined, or anticipated loss of love, safety, security, positive regard, control, certainty, or well-being

- Disciplined focus: the ability to concentrate on what you want to happen in any circumstance

- Accelerated learning: the ability to quickly process data in a nonjudgmental manner

- The E factor: the ability to maintain a mind-set of success and a focus on what is needed to be more successful

Nemerouf's premise is that what you create in life illustrates what you stand for. With increased awareness, you will know who you are and what you aspire to. And you will recover more rapidly from a negative triggered state the more you are entrenched in the other three positive factors and the more focused you are on your positive traits.

Triggered-State Recovery

At one point in the presentation Nemerouf asked for volunteers from the audience. The group quickly volunteered me as the sacrificial lamb. (They had learned the fine art of delegating!) He divided the sixteen participants into small groups and asked them to discuss and record those characteristics that described me consistently relative to their past and present experience of me. He would then compile their findings.

Here is Nemerouf's report, to which he appended his own charge.

> Ole,
> An understanding and magnetic
> presence, caring, passionate, sensitive,
> with a generous heart.

He provides the safety for others
to access and discover things
about themselves they
never thought possible.

A dear, loyal, and trusted friend
who is lovingly engaged with
those he cares about.

He knows when and how to hold
other people's feet to the fire.

Ole, this is your "gift." It is a reflection of who you
are and what you are truly dedicated to. The only
times you are distant from this gift is when you are
triggered. The faster you recover from a triggered
state, the more your gift is in full bloom.

Warm regards,

Nikki Nemerouf

What triggers me is when I sense that I am being controlled or
dismissed. The dark side can appear rapidly as I attempt to defend
my position or discard any constructive feedback. I return to being a
loner driven by conditioned needs and past beliefs of autonomy and
independence. That triggered state launches instantly, usually as some
form of flight, leaving my gift in the trash. That strategy served me
well during a period in my life, but not in all circumstances, and it
most likely will not serve me well in the future.

The alternative strategy for me to reflect on when I'm triggered is
to return to what Nemerouf refers to as my gift. If I draw upon my
strengths, I can then move forward in my life. I can be engaged with
my world and fears in a positive manner rather than being stuck in an
unproductive state. To successfully tap back into my gift takes aware-

ness and a conscious shift. It is not always easy, and it's not always fun. My ego and my triggered state scream for recognition, but ignoring them by shifting focus from the negative to the positive is necessary if I aspire to evolve.

Disciplined Focus

The life that you have created will reveal what you believe in and what you are committed to. The evidence is all around you, and it provides you with a mirror in which your core beliefs, assumptions, and past conditioning are reflected.

Are you working on your ability to concentrate on what you want to see happen in any given circumstance? If you truly focus on and believe in abundance, your bank account will be full and your future financially secure. If you sincerely believe that you deserve to be in a loving and connected relationship, you will be. If you believe that you are in control of your destiny, you will reject the notion of being a martyr or a victim or of remaining entrenched in your current negative role. If your life is filled with disappointments and setbacks, you are focused on a core belief that is creating those outcomes. Change the belief and change your focus and you will, over time, change the result.

As you read in chapter 3, the key to creating a remarkable life is to release oneself from the bondage of those core beliefs and basic assumptions that are roadblocks to realizing a life of fulfillment, gratitude, and joy. Queuing up in gigantic numbers just outside the borders of your consciousness is everything within reason that you have ever aspired to have. Everything! Open the gate and let it all in. It is the *more* that you have been seeking.

I used to believe, for example, that "money is the root of all evil." It was a conditioned belief that I acquired from being a member of the Carlson family. That unconscious belief prevented me from enjoying the benefits of economic freedom. I had to first become aware of that belief, evaluate objectively the negative consequences of continuing to hold that belief, and then use the tools in this book to see the Universe as a plentiful and bountiful place. Once that transformation took place, abundance came into my life and I believed that I deserved it. Analyze and alter your core beliefs and you free the gifts of the Universe that have been held in reserve by you, not by others. You, not some deity, your parents, society, or a warden of some external institution, are the gatekeeper. This is not the time to be stubborn and to cling to the past. You may need to re-engineer your beliefs and assumptions if what you aspire to is not in your life. It is time to be aware of all the unlimited possibilities that await you. It is time to put into practice the four attributes that make leaders flourish. Wake up, be aware, and gain control of your life. Make it remarkable.

FORGET THE NEED TO BE RIGHT

Living in Seattle during the 1970s, I listened habitually to an afternoon radio talk show hosted by psychologist Dr. Jennifer James. It was drive-time pop-therapy entertainment at its best. I was a devoted fan because of the combination of good advice, voyeurism, and the relief that I did not have the problems of those wretched souls dialing in for free advice.

I often heard Dr. James challenge her troubled callers by asking, "Would you rather be right, or would you rather be happy? You can't be both." (My version of that question would be "Would you rather be right, or would you rather be at peace with yourself and the Universe?") I never understood fully what Dr. James meant by that comment. I was a clueless, busy, young salesperson on autopilot, navigating my way home to my wife, kids, and a lawn that needed to be mowed. But now, I get it.

Coming from a position of being right requires an abundance of energy, righteousness, defensiveness, arrogance, judgment, prejudice, and narrow-mindedness. It leaves little open space for discussion, other points of view, options, or learning. When you are right, you are the expert. Period. You view yourself as superior to others only to find out as time passes and data expand that your self-anointed or academically accredited expertise is outdated. New information replaces what you defended so staunchly as the absolute truth. Welcome to the Information Age!

Newtonian physics has been replaced in the last one hundred–plus years by quantum physics. The electron microscope has revealed that matter apparently is not solid at all: It is energy in perpetual motion eventually compressed into nothingness. Wow, nothingness! All is nothing, invisible, and empty, yet we can touch it, feel it, and be it.

Multiple spiritual belief systems and organized religions compete for devotees among the billions of people who inhabit our miniscule planet as it revolves in the vastness of outer space. Makes you feel kind of small, doesn't it? Who, then, has the right spiritual authority? How would they know if they did? Who has the absolute power, permission, and knowledge to state that their beliefs, their deity, their afterlife, their demons, their book, their rituals, and their robed leaders are superior to those of others?

Will I be fitted for wings and audition to play the harp, or will I be measured for fire-absorbent red long johns and be vulnerable to sharp pitchforks? Will I come back again and again to learn the lessons required for my evolution to perfection and Nirvana? Will I pass through a long dark tunnel illuminated brilliantly at the end, where my past loved ones are waiting for me, or will the lights just suddenly go off with a "that's all folks"?

It appears to me that there are simply too many options on this planet to claim that one is the right one. We will all discover whether our truths are valid at the end of our particular physical and spiritual journeys. That is the one absolute experience and the one assurance that we can all agree upon. At that juncture it will not matter which discipline controls our thinking and actions. But that is why living in the present, in the now, is so vital. The world has continually been at war defending regional sacred and secular beliefs, and where has it gotten the human race? You do not need to do the research to know that death, destruction, and separation have been the consistent results.

According to a study released in February 2008 by the Pew Forum on Religion & Public Life, the fastest-growing segment regarding religion in the United States is the *nones*—not the nuns. Sixteen percent of the adult population claims to be unaffiliated with any religious organization, and 25 percent of Americans ages 18–29 report no religious affiliation at all. These populations are not necessarily atheist or agnostic; rather, they cannot conceive of any one religious dogma, deity, or traditional spiritual organization that captures in totality the divine and mysterious nature of creation, eternity, and the ultimate answers of life, death, and beyond. The territory is too vast. The possibilities are too many, the options too varied, and the opinions too strong to make a decision without evidence.

Responding to the Pew Forum Survey, Stephen Prothero, chair of the Department of Religion at Boston University states in an article in *USA Today* titled "American Faith: A Work in Progress," "The story behind the numbers of the latest survey is not that religion is in trouble. It is that religion is morphing into something new."

Open your eyes, your mind, your awareness, and your inherent reasoning to what is possible rather than to ancient beliefs and myths that have been accepted and followed because of fear, conditioning, and blind faith. What seems sensible to me is universal connectivity, not secular separation and division. Just as I said in chapter 2 when I introduced the concept of the Universe, you can define "your Universe" as a religion, spiritual preference, a higher power, or whatever you please, but consider that there is something greater and more powerful working in conjunction *with* you, not *against* you. It is a force that unites rather than divides. It is a wonder that is more mysterious and loving than definable, absolute, and fearsome. Consider the Universe to be an energy that participates in bringing to you what you aspire to be, do, and have.

The Earth is not flat and it is not the center of the solar system. Space is vast and infinite. The potential to be misinformed or proven wrong is endless and accelerating at warp speed. Being right sets you up for eventual disappointment, defensiveness, frustration, and stress. With investigation, you can find other options to your views about how the world works, how wealth is accumulated, what causes relationships to flourish, what to do to improve your health, and how immortality is or is not assured. These alternative views are just outside your awareness. People tend to go with what they know. Learn and be open to more.

On a much simpler level, I'm still trying to figure out whether or not coffee is good for me. Should I drink four glasses of milk daily, and is bottled water better for me than tap water? Remember the days when, as kids, we drank water from the rubber garden hose? Everyone's afraid to do that today, yet I am still alive and thriving. What is the right way to parent? Is Dr. Spock still right, or are there other, more suitable, options? Who really knows what is the right way to do anything? Who has permission to make up the rules and standards by which to raise our children and direct our individual lives? Take a stand and stand for something that defines you and what you believe. If you do not, others will aggressively jump in to fill that role and assume the command position that you have relinquished. Trust your inner voice and judgment.

BE HAPPY

Being happy allows you to consider multiple opportunities. It frees you to open up so that you can learn, see other points of view, and consider alternatives without the stress of being proved wrong. Being happy shields you from embarrassment or having the rug pulled out from under your life's core. It removes you from both unhealthy and unproductive competition.

Being happy does not mean that you are void of beliefs and assumptions. It does not mean that you are a puppet on a string or blowing whichever way the wind directs you. Being happy does not mean that you are without conviction. But it does mean that you believe in a larger horizon and a bigger, more expansive window of opportunity. As Helen Keller, the first deaf-blind person to graduate from college, observed, "Many persons have a wrong idea of what constitutes real happiness. It is not obtained through self-gratification, but through fidelity to a worthy purpose." Happiness suggests that you have room for alternative points of view, that you allow options and alternatives, and that you learn to override rigidity of thought and action, as well as negative core beliefs and past conditioning.

Being happy means that you listen more than you speak, that you consider more than you dictate. It suggests that you remain more open than closed, and that you decide fairly and objectively. Being happy means that if other people disagree with you, you will not be devastated, frustrated, judgmental, or become terminally unhappy.

Nor will you throw dissenters out of your life at the first speed bump. Being happy creates opportunities to wish others well and to continue or alter relationships in a positive manner, despite conflicting opinions and beliefs. Are you right, or are you happy? Which choice have you made?

In any situation that may challenge your assumptions and core beliefs, ask yourself "Is it worth taking such a strong stand, investing so much energy and stamina, and putting so much at stake personally? What would I rather be, right or happy?" I am suggesting that you choose happiness over righteousness.

EXERCISES

- Identify what is working and what is not working in your life.

- Identify your gift. What triggers you and separates you from your gift? What price are you paying as a result of this separation? How aware are you when this is happening?

- Identify your core beliefs about money and abundance.

- Identify your core beliefs about health, well-being, the medical profession, and pharmaceuticals.

- Identify your core beliefs about relationships, marriage, parents, children, and family.

- Identify your core beliefs about spirituality, religion, metaphysics, dogma, and doctrine.

- Identify your core beliefs regarding what you desire and deserve to have in life.

- Identify your core beliefs about learning, education, open-mindedness, and alternative ideas.

- Identify your core beliefs regarding your profession, career alternatives, what brings you joy and satisfaction, and what provides you abundance.

- As you move forward in your life, what are your basic assumptions regarding your future and what is possible for you? Are you optimistic, pessimistic, well prepared, worried? Are you obediently stumbling forward marching to someone else's drum?

ESTABLISHING THE FUNDAMENTALS

CHAPTER 5

INSIDE THE PERIMETER

When your values are clear to you, making decisions becomes easier.

—ROY E. DISNEY
NEPHEW OF WORLD FAMOUS ANIMATOR WALT DISNEY

Values establish the exterior perimeter of your life that either confines you or expands more of what you aspire to be, do, and have. If you value honesty over niceness, then you will aspire to have more candid conversations with good intent. If one of your values is integrity, then you will aspire to keep your word with others. If you value listening, then you will focus on the other person instead of preparing to talk.

Values are created internally and set the external boundaries that allow you to make choices that are either beneficial to you (having been well intended) or, unfortunately, are detrimental. Values define who you are, what you stand for, and how others will reminisce about your life after you are gone. Your values will determine the manner in which you reach your vision, your mission, and your goals. Values are the starting point in the process of manifesting more of what you want more of—*now*. Deciding on your values requires considerable thought, exploration, and thorough introspection. It is a heavy, soul-searching assignment; you might have to make a courageous stand in direct conflict with past conditioning or the tribe that surrounds you.

You filter your reality and make decisions through these standards as they continue to distinguish your identity throughout your journey. Please keep the values you select few in number, high in impact, and in the best interest of making a positive contribution.

ALTER YOUR CORE VALUES

As they begin their trip toward adulthood, most young people obediently adopt and implement what they have inherited from the early influences in their lives, most likely their parents. There is little opportunity to question the wisdom or effectiveness of the elder generation's code until they reach their teens and enter into the independent and rebellious years. I believe that period can be an opportune time for a healthy dialogue, and a chance for young adults to reset what was at one time forced upon them.

As you approached adulthood (whatever that is and whenever that actually occurred), if you remained aware and became wiser, you were exposed to other considerations relative to what your core beliefs and values were. You hopefully made life-enhancing choices and eradicated or altered those beliefs and values that did not serve you or others constructively. If you didn't make that adjustment, you probably have gotten used to lying on a sofa spilling your guts out to a bored, $200-an-hour therapist.

I know firsthand that people have the capacity to change and to initiate their personal transformation. It is a gift that is inherent in our makeup. We are not necessarily victims of the past or held hostage by what was initially laid upon us unless we choose to be. There is no life sentence unless you roll over and succumb to what is. It requires wakefulness and watchfulness as well as mustering the courage to swim against the tide.

I encourage you to alter your core values if they are not contributing positively to your life and to the lives of others. If you do not consciously make those adjustments, then you are tossing yourself into the dumpster of victims, martyrs, the have-nots, and followers. You will be forgotten and dismissed appropriately. Where you came from does not dictate where you are going forever and ever. It is your choice. Choose wisely.

For most of us, the initial influencers of a value-guided life are our parents. If you read the dedication and chapter 1, I gave you a glimpse of my natural parents and my mentors, the Copes. I offer—without judgment or blame—the following story about being brought up in the Carlson family to illustrate the birthplace of the values that dominated the early days of my life.

The Carlson Family's Values

My father, Lyman Beardsley Carlson, was an only child who was adopted by working-class parents in Tacoma, Washington, in 1905 through a Midwest orphanage. He graduated from Stadium High School and attended a few semesters at Pacific Lutheran University in this blue-collar lumber town. He quit his academic pursuits and went to work performing numerous manual labor-oriented jobs to survive the Great Depression, as did many others during that period.

Lyman picked fruit in the apple orchards of Eastern Washington and played the drums and an assortment of other instruments in a local Tacoma dance band. He fished on commercial boats off the coast of Alaska and in Puget Sound and worked as a longshoreman in the ports of the Northwest. My father welded naval vessels during World War II, and he held a carpenters' union card. As a young boy, I was fascinated with his tool kit and his mysterious welder's mask.

My mother, Anna Ida Broman, was born in 1912, the middle child of first-generation immigrant Norwegians. She dropped out of high school and went to work as a telephone operator at the impressionable age of sixteen. She later worked as a clerk in various retail stores and in bakery and candy factory assembly lines, and she took in people's ironing. Ida kept her head down and focused only on her immediate work. She seldom looked up to envision a brighter future for herself or her family. She was the hardest worker I have ever encountered. To be hardworking was a value she lived by her entire life.

My parents met one night when Lyman was playing drums in a downtown Tacoma nightspot. The rest is a bit fuzzy. Nobody can agree on or was willing to share the actual truth, but it seems that they were married at some undetermined point in their relationship (anniversaries were always a bit vague and never celebrated). Lyman and Ida created three Carlson offspring between 1931 and 1943: Lolly, Judy, and Ole.

In 1946, Lyman was in his early forties, working as a welder in the U.S. Navy shipyard in Bremerton and providing a stable income for a family of five. Ida, in her mid-thirties, was at home with three kids. With that as a backdrop, we experienced an incident that rocked and shattered our fragile foundation of family values, which failed to hold us steadfast throughout it and its aftermath. That moment would come to define us as it rumbled, undeterred, toward our home, without any advance warning.

We lived in a modest Bainbridge Island waterfront home, a home my father had remodeled and loved. In the winter of 1946 the area was deluged with weeks of heavy rain. The water-saturated ground on the steep bank that hovered menacingly above our house shifted. In a moment, in the darkness of night, tons of water-soaked earth, trees, and debris were released explosively from the hillside. Our home and all the other tangible possessions that lay in the landslide's path were destroyed.

Awakened by the roar, four of us escaped from the devastation caused by the dirt, trees, and debris, but five-year-old sister Judy was buried beneath the descending mud and branches. Lyman heard her muffled cries. She was kept barely alive trapped in an air pocket under a huge stump whose finger-like roots hovered protectively over her. With tears, sweat, and rain streaming down his mud-caked face, my father, with his bare, bleeding hands, frantically dug her out, scoop by scoop, removing the suffocating debris until she was free and in her mother's arms. I was three years old and remember none of it.

That evening, the Carlson family was literally left out in the cold. Shivering in our soaked pajamas and collectively in a state of shock, we waited for help to arrive. Survival was becoming our family strategy. The night was long, wet, and forbidding. It was a prediction of things to come. Just before daybreak, with the help of the local Red Cross, we were moved to a vacant unit at the World War II housing projects of East Bremerton. It was to be our home for the next three years.

What follows is Judy's adult account of the incident, which draws from my oldest sister's memories as well as her own.

After that first week passed, Daddy decided he had better go back to our house and salvage what he could. Lolly went with him. Momma, Ole, and I stayed at the projects in East Bremerton. They drove slowly up to what was left of our home. The rains had passed and the water flow from the hill was just a trickle leaving little indication of the devastating flood of water, mud, and trees that had occurred just days earlier. Just the eroded riverbed that had targeted our home and possessions gave any evidence of what had occurred. The remaining structure leaned hard against the remaining trees like a frail old woman with a walker. The whole property below the eroded bluff looked bruised, beaten, and battered. It was a daunting indicator of what was to follow.

Lolly and Daddy turned away from the house and walked across the road to the boathouse on our dock. When they got to the end of the dock, they could see the boathouse door had been ripped off and the padlock on the storage area in the back of the boathouse was missing. Everything was gone. The boat, the motor, Daddy's tools, nothing remained. The house and all our possessions had been destroyed. And now someone just as menacing as the landslide had in the dark of night finished the job. Everything that we owned was gone as if we never existed.

Daddy and Lolly walked to the house next door, but found no one home. No witnesses. They returned to the car and got in. Lolly asked Daddy, "What are we going to do?" Daddy didn't answer. He lit up a Lucky Strike cigarette, stared straight ahead, and drove back to the projects in silence. Momma met them at the door and said, "The insurance company called. They are classifying the landslide as an act of God. That means they won't pay a cent." And they didn't. We were wiped out. Our lives together began to gather dark storm clouds, and hope silently slipped out the back door.

Lolly, Momma, and Daddy stood at the door without saying another word. Daddy turned away from them both and went to the cupboard; he reached in and took out a bottle of whiskey. He slowly opened that bottle and deliberately poured a full shot, and that was the beginning of a long, sad journey that would become the next phase of our lives.

In his classic song "American Pie," songwriter Don McLean captures what I believe my father must have felt. During that stormy tragic night, the music in all aspects of Lyman's life died. He was never the same. He was the only father of the Carlson clan I remember. I knew no other.

People often say in tragedies like ours that they were grateful nobody was killed or hurt seriously. We were grateful to be alive and physically uninjured. The more devastating hurt, however, is invisible. It is emotional and psychological, and it eternally scars the soul of some victims. Some people do later recover, repair, replace, or do without. My parents were not among that group. There was no stalwart set of family values to sustain us through the loss. As a couple, my parents never healed for their own sakes, nor for the sakes of their three innocent children.

Lyman chose nicotine, alcohol, silence, anger, and a dispirited view of life to ease his pain. I often found him gazing off into a future that he believed he could no longer create. He had numerous brushes with the law, usually due to his excessive drinking, and a few other misdemeanors from acting upon impulse rather than sane judgment.

Along with our tangible family possessions, my father also lost his faith in God, people of position, and powerful institutions that defining night. He often wondered out loud: "What kind of a God could have arbitrarily been so destructive and unfair? Why would a respectable and trusted insurance company subordinate itself to such a God? What the hell kind of people are they? Where is the fairness and justice in all of this?" He was left to answer all of those questions for himself, and the bottle was his most convenient and favored adviser. I stood by absorbing his questions and messages, initially shaping my view of the world. The experience ripped out my father's heart and his will to start over again. The rest of us were dragged along in lockstep and obedient fashion—for a while.

Lyman quit his job at the shipyard and became a night shift bartender in a tavern in downtown Bremerton frequented by sailors and the local professional baseball team. I would often find those characters passed out on our secondhand sofa when I woke up in the morning.

Lyman told me later in life that I was an unwanted burden. He never wanted to have more children after my oldest sister was born. I believe it was the talk of a disheartened man. In retrospect, we both deserved better.

Ida's post-landslide lifestyle was similar to Lyman's. She smoked and drank and ate an unhealthy diet. When my parents were not fighting and degrading one another in full view of their children, Ida escaped nightly into the black-and-white pages of crime magazines while Lyman snored away, passed out on the sofa.

Lolly informed me that it had not always been like what Judy and I experienced. She remembered good times. She was "Lolly-pops" and the apple of her father's eye. She had my parents for nearly ten uninterrupted, relatively happy and prosperous years before Judy came along. But then my oldest sister later had the rug pulled out from under her feet as the family that she knew deteriorated. She lost what she had had. Perhaps in many ways her loss was the most devastating and hurtful. I never knew the difference. I never lost anything. You only know what you know.

Over the years, as a family, we all had various minimum-wage jobs and contributed to the monthly income stream. We depended on state unemployment checks and borrowing from friends and relatives, who were never paid back, to get through the days. Regardless, we were consistently broke, dodging bill collectors and scrambling to pay the rent to those SOB landlords and catering to the whims of those rich corporate bosses.

Lyman was a con man of sorts. When I was thirteen years old, he convinced an auto dealer in Oak Harbor to allow him to test-drive a mint condition black 1951 previously owned Cadillac for a few hours under the guise that he was going to purchase it. That was entirely ridiculous because in no way could he afford such a car. In good faith, the car dealer allowed him a trial run. It was a crisp autumn Saturday morning in the Northwest and Lyman was excited for the opportunity to get behind the wheel of such a fine automobile. He had somehow secured two tickets to a NFL exhibition football game at Husky Stadium in Seattle. He was going to surprise me and take me to the game in the Cadillac. He had a good heart and, in his mind, noble intentions. He would drive the two hundred miles round trip to the ball game, return the Cadillac after hours to the dealer on Saturday, make up some plausible story about being late returning the car, and call it a day. He obviously thought he could get away with this scheme. If he did not, so what, no harm done and life goes on. I knew nothing of his plan, nor did Ida.

My father and I excitedly headed out to Seattle, and at about the eighty-five-mile mark, we rear-ended a pickup truck towing a small fishing boat with a twenty-five horsepower Evinrude outboard motor attached to the stern. The chain reaction was spectacular. The truck, with the driver's foot pressed firmly on the brake, stutter-stepped out into the intersection frantically trying to avoid any further collisions. The trailer sprung free from the trailer hitch and stabbed the truck's tailgate. The wooden boat crumpled and was thrown to the concrete like a Dixie Cup at a watering station during the running of the Boston Marathon. The Evinrude outboard motor crystallized as if someone had dipped it in liquid nitrogen and then struck it hard with a, well, with a fast-moving Cadillac. The right side of the Cadillac's hood had a perfect full impression of a twenty-five horse-power Evinrude outboard motor in it. I learned a new word regarding the male sexual organ from my father as we slammed into the trailer holding the boat.

Lyman was distraught, but nonetheless, we rallied and cleaned up the crime scene as quickly as possible before the police could arrive. We provided the victims with false information (I have no idea) and made the game by the end of the first quarter. After the game, Lyman sat for an hour in a roadside tavern contemplating how he was going to deal with this latest drama while I sat alone in the punctured Cadillac. We drove the remaining distance home in silence, Lyman nursing a six-pack of Rainier beer to ease his pain and me exploring the meaning of the new word that I had heard at impact. Was it a noun or a verb?

On Monday, he returned the car to an irate car dealer who pressed charges on Tuesday. The judge sentenced Lyman to thirty days in the Island County jail. Ida filed for divorce while Lyman was doing his time, and she was granted sole custody of Judy and me in addition to a restraining order against Lyman. Judy and I were left to deal with Ida and her pent-up irrational rage. One day while I was in school, a deputy sheriff escorted Lyman home to our tiny rental after serving his time. He quickly gathered his meager belongings and was given a courtesy ride to the Greyhound bus station.

On that afternoon, with no particular fanfare, my father simply vanished from my life. I did not see or hear from him for another six years. He and I moved on. It was abrupt. I became skilled at leaving events and people in the past by going numb and pretending that it and they did not matter. I thought at the time that the deputy should have also taken Ida and Judy, placed them somewhere at their request, and dropped me off at the Copes. That would have worked.

Two years later, Judy found Bill the sailor at Ault Field, the Naval Air Station on Whidbey Island. She married him and ran off to Northern California before she graduated from high school. I was accustomed to that strategy, as Lolly had done essentially the same thing years earlier, only it was Zeke the airman from McChord Air Force Base when we lived in Tacoma. Judy immediately became pregnant, gave birth to Danny, divorced Bill, and then proceeded to marry Lyman "knock offs" two times in a row in order to reconcile her past relationship with her father. It never worked.

She finally came to her senses after struggling all those years. With the guidance of a good therapist, she gave up on the tactics she had tried, and she shed a view of life she had inherited through uninvited circumstances. Eventually she took control of her life and became the founder and CEO of a start-up bank that funds low-income housing. She became both a pioneer and a rock star in her industry. She is now emotionally healthy and doing much better as a single, retired, successful banker. I stay in touch with Judy, but not with Lolly. It is too stressful, and we have little in common except that we came from the same womb.

Ida and I became roommates—and agreed to tolerate one another—until I graduated from high school in 1962. We led separate lives and stayed out of one another's way. I took care of my needs. She took care of hers.

I created the opportunity to attend college and accepted a full football/academic scholarship to the University of Washington after a one-year stint at the United States Air Force Academy Prep School in Colorado Springs, Colorado. Ida relocated to Tacoma and the familiarity of the mind-numbing candy factory assembly line. She later married another alcoholic she met at a neighborhood tavern. He and I had nothing in common. I stayed away. Once was enough.

I learned from my parents to value and be guided by the negatives of life. These ingrained traits did not dominate my life all of the time, but they were my initial standards, and they were highly visible as I grew into adulthood. It was difficult and often confusing to distinguish what was the right thing to do. Parents have a profound influence upon their children. To give you specific examples would fill volumes. Some situations were horrific or, depending upon the vantage point, quite funny, filled with dark gallows humor.

We were collectively a self-inflicted train wreck—people trying to survive individually in a hostile and combative world that we attracted. It was everyone for him- or herself. The pain we imposed upon one another was often cruel, unjustified, and seldom apologized for. We just moved on, leaving a wake of failure and destruction in our rearview mirrors.

HOW I ALTERED MY CORE VALUES

As a child, I learned to be self-sufficient, trust few people—especially authority figures—and look out for "number one," sometimes at the expense of others. I cannot remember ever being told by my parents that I was loved or valued. Never. Later in life I fell back on that conditioning as I became more aloof, independent, and unsure of my worthiness and who I really was. It was the world that I lived in and what I knew.

I learned from my parents to discredit what had made many people successful. I had to experience those attributes elsewhere, and my radar was scanning the area. Enter Helen and Paul Cope. I dedicated this book to them because they gave me my first look at living a life entirely unlike the one I had become familiar with.

I mentioned earlier that we were living in Oak Harbor, Washington, when I entered high school. We had moved there from the mean streets of East Los Angeles—the Bell Gardens district—California, when I was ten years old. Our family settled initially into a tiny, dilapidated two-room apartment above Ronhaar's funeral parlor. No view.

We soon became familiar with the startling stench of formaldehyde that penetrated the thin linoleum-coated floorboards of our unit. We were attuned to the late-night intrusion of the resident undertaker firing up the engine of his outdated and menacing *Sleepy Hollow* black hearse to go pick up the newly departed. He would return with his one-time customer, back up the hearse beneath the overhanging garage roof, and unload the body into the embalming laboratory in the funeral parlor. We were thus some of the first to know when anyone in Oak Harbor had kicked the bucket.

We were dirt broke and had no vision for the future except to survive another twenty-four hours and not do further damage to one another. The intimidating hearse and the coffin display room were a constant reminder that our eventual fate was conveniently located just ten steps down a dark, unnerving, and crooked staircase. The dangling lightbulb that illuminated the stairwell frequently burned out, adding to the spookiness of the whole adventure of navigating up and down those creaky steps.

Helen and Paul's two sons, Jim and Paul, were classmates of mine from fifth through twelfth grades. Those years found me gravitating to their solid brick home, located on an oak tree–lined Norman Rockwell–like street, both before and after school. The Cope boys had everything that was missing from my life. They were valued, loved, and cared for. I claimed them as my own brothers and loved them as such.

It was both ideal and unfamiliar. I was trying to sort it all out. The gap between our families was enormous. I assumed that if I hung around long enough, stayed friends with Jim and Paul, and caused little trouble, the Copes would extend to me an invitation to be a part of their family—one which I viewed to be of the idyllic fifties *Father Knows Best* variety. I was little different from an abandoned cat, a sort of stray that hung out, meowed, and purred just loudly and persistently enough at the doors of this home to be fed, sheltered, and taken in. Once inside, I was never asked to leave, nor wanting to vacate for better digs and perks.

I was given unconditional love by all four Copes. They included me in summer boating vacations and offered unsolicited parental advice. I had my own twin bed—with clean sheets—in Paul Junior's bedroom whenever I wanted to stay over. Helen cooked great nutritious meals, and the family extended invitations to holiday celebrations. Ida and Lyman stayed out of the way—perhaps unaware or relieved that someone else was picking up the burden and tab. I was outsourcing myself.

WHAT DOESN'T KILL US MAKES US STRONGER

My launching pad for a healthy and productive life was tainted, but through self-awareness and the unsolicited intervention of others at pivotal points in my life, I often flourished and had intersections of success and enlightenment. My life has resembled a Wall Street mutual-fund chart over the past six decades: numerous peaks and valleys, but moving upward over the long term. Surprisingly, many of those early, hard-earned lessons of self-sufficiency and independence have served me in a positive manner. It was all that I knew and I was quick to adapt.

Several years ago a psychologist tested me. Among the ten thousand participants who had previously been profiled, no one had scored higher than I had in the category of autonomy and independence. I figured that it was something to boast about until the psychologist and I analyzed the test results and the consequences of continuing that behavior. He suggested that intimacy might be a better choice to move toward for the years remaining. That is my present journey, but it has been difficult to give up the familiar. Surviving in a family like mine provided the previous curriculum. It was essential that I took care of myself. Nobody else did. I am not chest-pounding proud of my heritage, yet I have an appreciation for the circumstances that shaped those outcomes.

I left what remained of the family at age eighteen and never returned. Ida died from Alzheimer's in her mid-sixties in a rest home; Lyman passed on at about the same age, living alone in a low-income apartment on Capital Hill in Seattle, succumbing to the eventual ravages of alcoholism.

My parents were and still remain a mystery to me. At various times we lived under the same roof, but we never really knew or understood one another or sustained anything of foundational value. Looking back, quite frankly, it was not all that bad. We only know what we know at the time we are in the experience. In some dark way it shaped who I am today, and I find some positive value in having been there and absorbed all that I did. Mine was a life experience that few of my fraternity brothers or the business executives I have worked with had in common with me.

I often fantasize how our life would have been had Lyman not made his choice to open the cabinet and reach for the bottle. The landslide defined him instead of him defining the landslide. He had no firm set of sustainable values that guided him throughout his entire life, especially not at that unexpected intersection where a difficult and a courageous choice had to be made. Lyman was not born an evil man.

He was a troubled man, often haunted by the fact that he was put up for adoption by his natural parents and the rejection that it represented to him. Perhaps he felt unloved at the core of his being. Later in life, he was simply sick with the devastating disease of alcoholism. He never recovered. Ida followed with her own version of rudderless values, allowing rage and desperation to dominate, and the dance began.

We are always going to experience our version of a landslide, be it a financial loss, an illness, the death of or separation from a loved one, or some personal setback. Most of us will survive and even prosper from that experience if we have thoughtfully and deliberately defined what our values are, what it is that we stand for. It is like that old axiom by eighteenth-century German philosopher Friedrich Nietzsche, "What doesn't kill you makes you stronger." It is imperative to have that solid foundation under you when your world begins to rock and tumble. Without a bedrock of sustainable life-enhancing values, the bottle, or your version of the bottle, must look inviting. It may seem like the only alternative available to you as you plunge into depths that seem impossible to overcome.

I do not know your background. Perhaps you got lucky and inherited from loving parents life-enhancing values with which to charter your course of life. Great! Keep on doing what has got you to where you are today. If you find yourself in the opposite position, I know that you can make better choices for yourself to receive what you really aspire to in life and what you truly deserve. Cast away what is getting in your way and reach out and harvest what others have that makes them successful. You can make that choice.

Study highly successful people and what they stand for. Most operate with a highly visible set of values that sustain them through good and troubled times. It is their code and the foundation of their success. It creates a filter through which they make life-enhancing choices, no matter what they define as their success. What do you stand for that allows you to create more in your life?

EXERCISES

- Who in your life do you most admire? What are the values that govern their lives? How do their values match up to yours? What evidence can you produce that verifies that they do?

- What values did you inherit that do not serve you in a positive manner? How willing are you to let them go and replace them with more constructive guidelines for your life? Where do you specifically need to make adjustments?

- State the values that you deem most important. What is your equivalent of the "ten commandments"?

- Identify specific instances when you took a stand and made your values visible to others.

- What follows is a list of core values. Circle the ones that resonate with you and guide your life's decisions and choices. Add any additional ones to the bottom of these columns.

Acceptance	Dedication	Graciousness
Accountability	Duty	Gratitude
Authenticity	Education	Happiness
Autonomy	Equality	Health
Career	Excellence	Independence
Caring	Fairness	Individualism
Community	Fame	Influence
Competency	Family	Inspiration
Competition	Forgiveness	Integrity
Creativity	Freedom	Joy
Credibility	Friendship	Justice

EXERCISES (CONTINUED)

Love	Redemption	Success
Originality	Relevance	Transparency
Passion	Respect	Trust
Peace	Responsibility	Trustworthiness
Power	Service	Truth
Recognition	Spirituality	Wealth
Reconciliation	Status	Wisdom

Review the list that you circled and narrow your choices to ten values that best define you or will lead you into the future. Now choose five that are nonnegotiable to be the hallmarks of your legacy. Your choices in life become simple to craft and implement when you start from a clearly stated set of values that are yours, not what someone branded you with.

CHAPTER 6

YOUR MOON

The most pathetic person in the world is someone
who has sight, but has no vision.

—HELEN KELLER
AMERICAN AUTHOR, ACTIVIST, AND LECTURER

Establish your personal vision of your remarkable future. This is the larger picture that you are moving toward. Focus on the end result, allowing the Universe and the powerful mechanisms of your mind to work out the finite details and all of the unforeseen twists and turns that are required to get there. Remember, you are teleological and will therefore self-correct en route to the target.

In 1961, President John F. Kennedy declared publicly that his vision for the United States of America's outer space program was to put a man on the Moon and return him safely to Earth by the end of the decade. It was an ambitious goal. He declared: "We choose to go to the Moon. We choose to go to the Moon in this decade and do the other things, not because they are easy, but because they are hard, because that goal will serve to organize and measure the best of our energies and skills, because that challenge is one that we are willing to accept, one we are unwilling to postpone, and one which we intend to win, and the others, too."

The implementers would be exploring the unknown, and many course corrections would therefore be needed along the way. The project was filled with uncertainty, doubt, and skepticism, but in spite of all the obstacles, JFK's goal was reached—with the help, of course, of the U.S. Treasury and a considerable number of dedicated and passionate experts.

What moon, essentially, are you aiming for? How committed are you to reaching it? Is your vision going to be a stretch, or are you aiming so low that it will be easy? Artist and inventor Michelangelo said, "The greater danger for most of us lies not in setting our aim too high and falling short, but in setting our aim too low, and achieving our mark." Who is in your corner? You may not have the financial support of the U.S. Treasury or a covey of experts at your beck and call. However, you do have access to other powerful resources and an immediate circle that will respond when notified of your intentions. Where do you want to go, be, do, and have regarding your mind, body, spirit, self, money, people, and balance of life?

It is essential to create significant and equal balance between the tangible and intangible outcomes of your life. These outcomes cannot be mutually separated or in conflict with one other. Tangible visions and goals yield homes, cars, bulging bank accounts, beautiful jewelry, exotic vacations, and anything else that money can buy. They focus on the things you want to have more of that you can touch. They also represent what might be taken away from you in the event of a tax audit, a bankruptcy, or a divorce. A life that is fixated only on tangible goals may leave you with no internal reserves or no foundation from which to jump-start in case unforeseen tragedy occurs.

Balance your tangible vision regarding what you aspire to be and do and have more of with intangible aspirations as well. People will soon forget what you once owned, but all their lives they will remember what you were to them, how you influenced them, and the legacy of happiness you left behind. Poet Linda Ellis speaks of this focus and eventual legacy in her poem "The Dash."

THE DASH

I read of a man who stood to speak
at the funeral of a friend.
He referred to the dates on her tombstone
From beginning—to the end.

He noted that first came the date of her birth
And spoke of the following date with tears.
But he said what mattered most of all
Was the dash between those years.

For the dash represents all the time
That she spent alive on earth . . .
And now only those who loved her
Know what that little line is worth.

For it matters not how much we own:
The cars . . . the house . . . the cash.
What matters is how we live and love
And how we spend our dash.

So think about this long and hard . . .
Are there things you'd like to change?
For you never know how much time is left
(You could be at "dash mid-range.")

If we could just slow down enough
To consider what's true and real,
And always try to understand
The way other people feel.

And be less quick to anger,
And show appreciation more
And love the people in our lives
Like we never loved before.

If we treat each other with respect,
And more often wear a smile . . .
Remembering that this special dash
Might only last a little while.

So when your eulogy's being read
With your life actions to rehash . . .
Would you be proud of the things they say
About how you spent your dash?

How do you want to spend your dash? What do you want to be proud of when your life is rehashed?

What do I aspire to have more of in my life? I insist, with appropriate consideration and intent, on defining and doing what satisfies and fulfills me for greater mutual benefit. I want to leave a legacy that speaks of aliveness, contribution, and uniqueness. I want to ride my rocket to where I aspire to go. I intend to leave a mark that defines me in the hearts, minds, and spirits of those I influenced, inspired, and transformed. "He was here making a difference," they will say, "and we are better off for being here with him."

As my friend and former pro-football player Gary Tofil reminds me, "Playing defense, mailing it in, or sitting on the sidelines just doesn't hack it. Play ball, or get off the field!" That is also a driving force in my vision.

I wish for you similar aspirations—that you become the master of your life. We can take the journey together. Author James Michener wrote the following: "The master in the art of living makes little distinction between his work and his play, his labor and his leisure, his mind and his body, his information and his recreation, his love and his religion. He hardly knows which is which. He simply pursues his vision of excellence at whatever he does, leaving others to decide whether he is working or playing. To him he's always doing both."

It might strike you as selfish, somewhat arrogant, or even a little self-absorbed to take such a position in life as Michener and I suggest. That is for you to determine. If you remain conscious, you might discover that the voice you hear whispering those judgments comes from the conditioned recesses of your past that recommend safety, conformity, sacrifice, victimization, and even martyrdom as noble and appropriate life strategies. The voice might suddenly launch when you are tempted to deviate from the norms set by families, religions, governments, peers, educational institutions, traditions, customs, and codes. When similar impulses infiltrate my awareness, I know that I am about to "vanilla-ize" my life and vanish into the crowd. Before you succumb to the momentum that will carry you down a well-trodden, familiar path, resist by turning down the volume and switching channels to allow a wiser voice to speak to you. I want you to go where the queue is short and the visions are far-reaching and beyond established reasonableness.

Here is the challenge: Dare something that is remarkable. Dare something that is meaningful to you. Dare something for the betterment of the planet without asking anything in return. Your return will come to you in untraditional ways. You will automatically differentiate yourself from the masses. Dare something that may seem beyond your immediate reach; make it far beyond the hopes and dreams of your traditional tribe. Go ahead and screw up the curve. Dare something that may scare the daylights out of you and those surrounding you. Dare to claim your unique greatness, shedding any self-imposed or invasive limiting core beliefs of your past that have been holding you and your future in reserve. Get off the bench and play!

CREATE YOUR VISION OF THE FUTURE

Whoever you are, whatever you have, and whatever you are doing is a direct result of your past and current visions. Your success or discontent is merely a mirror of your vision, conditioning, and core beliefs. If that destination and accumulation are all that you desire from life and they are serving you and others well, then you deserve a pat on the back. You are on a good, forward path and have figured things out.

If you are off target and falling short of your expectations, pay attention, because something is amiss and it is up to you to make the change. "But that cannot be," you tell yourself and others indignantly, "because I envision my life overflowing with prosperity, great health, superstar status, loving relationships, and adventurous travel. I affirm obediently the detailed outcomes I wrote on my 5 × 7 multicolored index cards. I have watched *The Secret* DVD twelve times. I have read *The Secret* too, earmarking important passages, and I've attended weekly focus and discussion groups. I am a talking, walking, positive-thinking, affirming, visualizing, emoting, vibrating, energy-broadcasting maniac."

Take another look. The reality you are experiencing is that you are in credit card or student loan debt up to your private parts and not making any loan-reduction progress. Bummer! The text-messaging Gen Yers are passing you by at the office. And your marriage is in the files of a divorce lawyer. It's not working! Hmmm. It's time to play detective again. Where are your fingerprints at these crime scenes? Step over the yellow tape; carefully examine the chalk silhouette of what is not working in your immediate life, and initiate alternate choices. If you don't, you'll be stuck with what you have.

Is there a chronic disparity between your current vision and the results that you are experiencing? The culprit, most likely, is not your vision; it is the incredible power in your subconscious mind and the programming you received as a youngster. The pertinent, important question, then, is what are you going to do next to transcend that influence and thus change your existing unacceptable situation?

Your subconscious, self-limiting core beliefs and conditioning have hijacked you and have overridden your present intentions. You need to go to work on the fundamentals: Examine and alter your core beliefs about life and create a better foundation for your vision. If you do not make a better decision, the decision will be made for you. Your launching pad will become unstable. Perhaps you did not ask for this; you showed up and got dealt a crummy hand. Take heart. You can fix this, but it will take some focus, effort, and perhaps a whole lot of ego reduction, forgiving, understanding, and reconciliation. It might take longer than you expected.

Let's begin by putting some intentional, well-intended future-vision stakes in the sand and see what happens. One of the guidelines in this process is to remain in balance. Your stakes need to be spread out, incorporating a total picture of your life—not just focusing on one familiar and comfortable aspect of your life or something that you are desperately lacking. I have discovered that the more in balance you are, the higher your success rate in achieving your vision and reaching your individual goals. You will avoid burnout and setting yourself up for a devastating experience should you have a setback in the primary facet that you have chosen for yourself. For instance, if you identify primarily as being the matriarch of the family (mom/grandmother), when the kids grow up and leave to go to college, get married, or escape in some other way from you and your ways, you might have a difficult time adjusting. Now no one desperately needs you.

If your primary identity is being the founder/CEO/president of a flourishing business and the business is sold, you might be feeling a bit empty as you take out the family garbage and pour your own cup of ordinary coffee in the morning. Candidly speaking (work with me on this), having substantial funds from selling a financially success-ful business and not having to spend that money on kids (they are change-the-locks gone) sounds fine to me, but maybe not to others. Picture this: chasing your spouse around a paid-off house, giggling and laughing, anytime you want, with no money concerns! These events and occurrences—kids gone, business sold—are somewhat neutral; it is how you respond to them that will make the difference in your life.

There are many facets of your life to choose from as you create your future vision. Here are a few areas to consider as you strive for the balance I spoke of earlier. You are free to add your own.

Mental and physical health

Spiritualism/religion

Relationships/people

Wealth/prosperity

Career/professional

Self/personal

Learning/mind

What do you want to achieve in the future in these and other categories? Take your time, be thoughtful, and give yourself permis-sion to stretch your vision beyond what is familiar. Write down your thoughts and aspirations in your journal, and let them incubate, but not for too long.

Let me share my vision with you at this point in our discussion. My vision is always a work-in-progress, just as yours will be. I have edited some of the statements for personal and confidentiality reasons, but essentially this is what I am working on and moving toward as of the writing of this book. I want to give you a real example—not an academic, theoretical, or philosophical template. I have specific goals and affirmations that support this vision. Those goals and their accompanying affirmations are written on the reverse side of the corresponding vision index card for each category. This ensures that everything is clear, focused, and in alignment. (In chapters 8 and 9 I will show you what is written on the reverse side of these cards so you can see the complete process.)

I write and revise my vision using my laptop and printer (my handwriting is not very legible) on white, unlined 5 x 7 index cards. I travel a great deal, and the cards need to move easily with me in a laptop case or briefcase. You can handwrite them or configure your computer and printer to produce them.

SPIRITUAL

I am a spiritual entity. I am complete, healthy, perfect, robust, powerful, loving, balanced, and joyful. I affirm and actualize my powerful vision daily. My positive thoughts, words, mental pictures, and emotions determine my reality. The Universe brings all good things to me and supports me in all that I do. The Universe meets all of my needs immediately, and I am a magnet for all of my positive desires. I accept the gifts of the Universe with joy and gratitude. What I do not have now is on its way. Following are the indisputable facts of my life.

MIND AND BODY

I am in excellent mental and physical health. I exercise, think positively, and eat and drink in a healthy manner. I take supplements to keep me healthy, strong, and alert. My thoughts, words, mental pictures, and emotions are positive and focused. I respond to all situations in a calm, positive, and thoughtful manner. My body is strong, resilient, relaxed, lean, flexible, rested, and youthful. I live a healthy and active life.

ABUNDANCE

I live in an abundant Universe. I create, accept, and deserve wealth. I am financially secure and independent. My unlimited wealth comes from speaking, writing, consulting, training, investments, online and back-of-the-room product sales, Social Security, and other resources of the Universe. I am wealthy, prosperous, and abundant. With joy and gratitude I share this abundance with others.

PERSONAL

On the road and at home, I play golf, exercise, play my guitar, eat healthfully, write, create products, read, watch TV, and attend plays, concerts, movies, and sporting events. I hang out with my wife, rest, dine out, and visit with friends and family. I enjoy cooking and entertaining. I treasure all aspects of my life.

PEOPLE

I love others and myself unconditionally. I attract positive, successful, joyful, and grateful people. I am a loving husband, father, relative, friend, and colleague. I am connected to a greater community and interact with this "tribe" with immaculate intent. I value my relationships and continually strive to make them better.

PROFESSIONAL VISION

I influence those who influence many. I am a world-class keynote speaker, corporate trainer, strategic-planning consultant, and a renowned published author. My partner and I are a team. I outsource appropriate tasks to keep the business simple. Advocates advise me and I accept their support and implement their ideas successfully. I attend seminars to improve my professional skills. I develop new material, products, and content, and remain highly visible. I am an articulate, humorous, passionate, engaged, present, entertaining, knowledgeable,

and stylish speaker. My presence, staging, audiovisuals, products, and content have an extraordinary impact. My writing is clear, concise, accurate, entertaining, thought provoking, and intelligent. I appear on talk shows and have positive articles and reviews from clients and the media.

THE CARLSON MANIFESTATION PROCESS

The following process is what I do to transform and translate my vision into my current reality. It works for me. Be creative and customize the steps for yourself. Experiment with the process and adapt it to what works best for you regarding style and methodology. We are all uniquely different, and what works for one person may not work for you.

1. Balance is key and essential. Let your ideas incubate over a period of time. Make your vision a stretch from where you are now. You have the rest of your life to implement your vision. As you write down your vision, allow yourself some white space to sort out what is really important to you. What will bring you joy, and what will you be grateful for having in your life?

2. I write my vision in affirmative language. That means it is personal (I use the pronouns I, me, mine), it is positive (I stay focused on the future), and it is in the present tense (I write as if I already have the vision in my life). Use simple yet exciting and imaginative vocabulary. Be explicit and clear. If you want more abundance in your life, name the figure. "My net worth is five million dollars."

3. I affirm how I want my life to be, not how it is or how it was, if there is any disparity. I am "future pacing" myself, riding the energy and momentum toward my vision. Future pacing simply means "setting future targets for myself to accelerate toward." Write your vision in a positive, forward-looking direction. If you desire more prosperity in your life, do not affirm that you are no longer broke. Affirm that you are abundant, wealthy, and deserve to have prosperity in your life.

4. I tweak my vision often. That is my style; it satisfies my need for constant change and innovation.

5. I am diligent about noticing the signs of progress as I move toward my vision. The results of your vision may not come to you all at once. The Universe may give it to you piecemeal, and you need to be alert to those partial offerings because they are often stepping-stones to the entire package.

6. Sometimes adjustments, course corrections, and additional actions are required. I incorporate these amendments into my vision as they arise. Stay awake, be flexible, and act upon the new information.

Now allow me to explain the daily rituals that keep me focused on my vision.

Each morning (usually about 5:00 AM—I love the morning), to set the tone for that day, I plug my Bose noise-reduction earphones into my laptop, bring up iTunes, and then select and play preprogrammed meditative music. I try to do this wherever I am—at home, in a hotel, or on vacation. I do so faithfully because it relaxes me. As I am listening to the music, I read aloud my vision from the index cards. I imprint my future into my subconscious mind and broadcast it out to a vast and receptive Universe. The vision creates vivid mental pictures and powerful positive feelings; the music creates a receptive mood and rhythm. As I progress through the cards, I take my time. I don't rush or force this portion of the routine. This is a dynamic, evaluative exercise for me. I reload parts of the vision that I have reached with new outcomes, or I eliminate elements of the vision that, after due consideration, I no longer deem important.

This meditative process takes from ten to fifteen minutes in the quiet, uninterrupted stillness of the morning. I have invested in my future and proactively set in motion my vision, thus attracting to me what it is that I desire.

I am not maniacal about this process. If I do miss a morning, I might perform this meditative ritual in the evening, or while sitting on an airplane (earphones are a must), or the next day as my driver takes me to the hotel from the airport. The only restriction is that it's best not to read your vision aloud in these situations.

AVOID THESE TRAPS

Just as there are positive rituals to try to practice every day, there are negative rituals—traps, really—that you should avoid as much as possible.

1. Frantically waking up with a jolt to an intrusive alarm clock or radio. Starting your day by catapulting yourself out of bed and immediately listening to or watching early morning breaking-news programs.

2. Washing down a sugarcoated, fat-saturated donut, or a bagel or two, with four cups of caffeine-injected coffee or an off-the-shelf power drink or fruit juice.

3. Creating on the run an emergency to-do list for the day that is completely short term and shows no respect for the long-term life that you deserve to live.

4. Air-kissing from a distance your loved ones as you dash out the door to whatever your hurried task list dictates is important to you for that day.

5. Setting in motion with the Universe a reactive, stressful, and repetitive day. The Universe will deliver objectively, without judgment, the waste that you are affirming. Waste or value?

Remember, the choice is yours; there's no room for finger-pointing.

Maharishi Mahesh Yogi, founder of Transcendental Meditation, recognized that "the human physiology is part of the cosmic physiology. Every rhythm of the universe therefore naturally has an effect on the individual and vice versa." We are multifaceted, multidimensional, interconnected spiritual beings swirling about in a vast and powerful Universe, affecting one another with our individual thoughts, mental pictures, and emotions. There is no isolation; no individual cells are operating outside and independent of one another. There is only connectedness, and you deserve to be connected to what brings you fulfillment, satisfaction, peace, and abundance. You deserve all that you desire to make you whole, connected, and complete. Start your day by engaging with the Universe and putting your mind in a positive, life-enhancing partnership with it. To use a modern term, you are partnering with the Universe in a co-pay arrangement. If you don't become a partner, you will surely lose ground. Give yourself a chance. Be in charge, and take the initiative. If you don't, others will.

Your vision for your future will be an alphabet soup of your standards, desired outcomes, dreams, core beliefs, spiritual orientation, past conditioning, and current desires. Let the Universe know what to deliver; be alert and willing to implement alternative strategies and actions when necessary.

EXERCISES

- Examine what is working in your life and explore the core beliefs that you hold regarding reaching those positive outcomes. Keep affirming those beliefs. Write them in your journal. Experience how you feel as you focus on what is working.

- Examine what is not working in your life and explore the core beliefs that you hold regarding reaching those negative outcomes. You may have to dig deep underneath the surface or have a conversation with a trusted friend to uncover the beliefs. Examine how you feel when focusing on those beliefs and outcomes. Write them in your journal.

- Isolate the core beliefs that are holding you back and reverse them. For example, if one of your current core beliefs is "I believe that money is the root of all evil," the result in your life could be that you struggle with your finances and consistently sabotage your financial well-being. Reverse that current core belief to say, "I believe that wealth, prosperity, and abundance provide financial freedom and happiness." Or "I easily create, accept, and deserve unlimited wealth." Affirm that belief as if you already held it. Write it in your journal.

- Choose the categories that you want to expand in your life: professional, relationships, spirituality, abundance, health, etc. Remember, stay in balance. Write the name of each of those categories at the top of a page in your journal and begin to fill in the outcomes that you desire below each heading. Stretch! Be explicit.

EXERCISES (CONTINUED)

- Identify the core beliefs that you will need to hold in order to reach the outcomes in the chosen categories. If your core beliefs do not support the outcomes, change the beliefs. Write the new beliefs in your journal and begin affirming them as if you already believed them.

- Over time, solidify your visions and organize them in somewhat the same fashion that I demonstrated earlier. Begin your ritual of imprinting and broadcasting your vision to your subconscious and to the Universe. Follow the guidelines initially, and then make any appropriate course corrections that work for you.

CHAPTER 7

STAY ON YOUR RED CARPET

*Here is the test to find [out] whether your mission
on earth is finished: If you're alive, it isn't.*

**—RICHARD BACH
AMERICAN SELF-HELP WRITER**

My purpose—or mission, if you prefer—in life is to influence those who influence many. This purpose defines on a daily basis where I should focus my energy and intentions. If what I am doing is not on purpose, then why do it? I don't, most of the time, but the temptation is always present.

Your purpose will be your North Star that guides and influences how you reach your future vision. It is the voice that whispers to you which path to take to remain aligned with who you are, what you want to accomplish, what your legacy will be, and how to be consistent with your defining standards.

HOW I FOUND MY PURPOSE—OR HOW MY PURPOSE FOUND ME

I struggled for years to determine what my purpose should be and how it would direct me into the future. After attending seminars, reading countless self-help books, and listening to CDs and audiotapes, I would occasionally declare a position because it sounded good or because it might impress others, but nothing resonated with me. I was attempting to please others at the expense of not pleasing myself, similar to Maria Shriver's journey. As a result, I bounced around, confused and unfulfilled in my professional life, never tethering myself to a noble internal purpose that would make a significant difference to me, or to others. The world at large was never a consideration. It never occurred to me to create a personal purpose statement, to create a one-stop, celestial covenant with the Universe that would connect me with everything that really mattered to me. I was frustrated, tied to an unconscious strategy to remain unconnected to why I was here.

I held numerous positions in many companies in multiple industries, but I never quite connected in any significant manner to anything that I was doing except providing an uneven and unpredictable revenue stream for myself and my family. I looked on with envy as my friends moved forward in their chosen callings, building their careers, expertise, futures, and net worth. Many had already decided what they wanted to be when they grew up; they had defined their purpose while attending institutions of higher learning. They became physicians, attorneys, business leaders, educators, dentists, coaches, spiritual leaders, and such. I don't know if they had composed personal purpose statements or not, but it appeared to me that they were on a defined path with intentional self-directed momentum.

In all honesty, my undeclared and implicit occupational purpose was to not be discovered for being the imposter that I believed that

I was. I felt like I had to keep changing careers before I was caught and exposed. I had little unique definition and hardly any constructive, intentional rationale to make any significant contribution. The results showed as I remained professionally uninspired and directionless, appearing to do well in life but never connected to an internal driving force or outcome. I was the proverbial ship without a rudder.

I worked for major public companies—Xerox, Morgan Stanley, CBRE—as well as small entrepreneurial concerns—an outdoor electrical advertising company and a country club developer. I showed up and performed just adequately enough to attract attention and have options. I personally created and invested in real estate partnerships, and I contracted as a trainer and facilitator for numerous training companies and an international CEO forum organization. I kept moving forward, sometimes horizontally, until it became clear that I was never going to qualify for and receive that corporate gold watch for long years of loyalty. Perhaps some of you can relate. Hang in there; the story gets better. I finally reached clarity and understood where I belonged and what I was meant to do, and you will too.

I sensed that there had to be more to life, but where could I find it? How could I engage at any meaningful level with it? Whatever "it" was remained a total mystery to me. I was passing through my professional life instead of being fully engaged with it. My purpose was implicit, weak, and leading me nowhere except toward a gradual downhill spiral. Unless you were inside my mind and heart at that time, you cannot imagine how dispiriting that situation was. I was comparing myself to others and being compared by others. I was lost.

On the personal side, I was providing for my family, being an acceptable citizen (no rap sheet), and remaining physically healthy. But mentally and spiritually I was out of sorts. I attempted organized religion, but I found myself unconnected and spiritually unfulfilled.

Observing people sleepwalking through religious services, and watching the evening news as yet another religious icon was reported as having fallen victim to temptation and fraud, separated me further from the dogma and the teachings that I thought I was supposed to adhere to.

Driven by my increasing frustration, I quit creating any purpose statements and waited patiently while affirming that my real path was on its way. I don't remember any specific self-help book or seminar that suggested that strategy, but it was an appropriate one. I had been clogging the pathway with my own lack of clarity, discipline, self-imposed confusion, and insincere intentions.

My purpose found me eventually when I least expected it. I did not discover or create it consciously through cognitive thinking, brainstorming, or consulting with an occupational counselor. I simply attracted my purpose to myself at a very unconscious level, and I was alert enough in my early forties to pounce on it once it was in my consciousness. The Universe was pounding loudly on my door with an incredible gift. I was given an opportunity to teach self-esteem, goal-setting seminars for a well-established national seminar company. The gift was offered and I grabbed it with unfamiliar energy and enthusiasm. Leading my first seminar at a resort in the foothills of Mt. Hood, Oregon, I knew immediately, at a spiritual level, that I was home and near my purpose. I could feel the internal shift. I was waking up and teaching others what I myself needed to learn. The abundance and numerous other opportunities would follow.

Soon afterward, in an overflow audience at an industry association conference, I listened to a gifted speaker lecture about the power of leverage and influencing leaders who had significant followings. Then it struck me: *That's it; he's talking directly to me. Why are these other people even here? He is teeing-up my purpose in life. I can become the one who influences those who influence many.* He actually said those words in passing, as part of the content of his speech, and the message did not pass by me. I heard that communication as if it were amplified through the speakers of some rock star's blow-the-doors-off sound system. If the stars lined up right, and I made some necessary adjustments, I could broadcast my message to successful leaders who would then broadcast it to their constituencies. Through influential individuals and teams, I could affect leaders and others. That was my audience. My purpose was there in place, waiting patiently for me to align with it.

Finally I had a specific direction and a defined purpose. I climbed on board, rode the newly found energy, and went to work at considerable financial risk and with some—okay, I admit, much—trepidation. With no noteworthy investment money, no expertise, no sustainable support from my immediate community, I dove into the deep end.

It was both exhilarating and humiliating. I threw up in a public restroom in Anchorage, Alaska, immediately before my first keynote address. Not pretty. I guess I was nervous about the whole experience. It was an embarrassing performance, but nobody died or went to jail. It took me three agonizing months before I mustered up enough courage to watch a videotape of a seminar I facilitated in Seattle. I felt my performance was awful, but I was on the field playing and getting in my repetitions. Tony Robbins says, "If you can't, you must." It was scary. All the demons of the past paraded across my consciousness every time I went before a crowd—he is shy, he slurs his words, he talks too fast, his enunciation is poor, he mispronounces words—but I kept persevering, moving toward the goal. My learning curve was steep, my fear was ever present, and I was not at all good, but my purpose was finally clear and pushing and pulling me forward.

During the journey, I lost my familiar past relationship with time and personal energy. Hours would pass as I worked on creating original material, and I hardly noticed. Nothing seemed like work as I had experienced it in the past. I was tirelessly dipping into a seemingly bottomless well of energy. It was a purpose on steroids, in the flow, in the zone, tapping into resources that seemed to come from everywhere at any given time.

For the first time in my life I felt no boundaries, only freedom. I feel it as I create this book. I began to understand what insurance giant and motivational author W. Clement Stone meant when he said, "When you discover your mission, you will feel its demand. It will fill you with enthusiasm and a burning desire to get to work on it."

I began to create authentic material, coach corporate leaders, write books, give keynote speeches to large international audiences, facilitate personal transformation seminars, and consult with companies regarding strategic plans and how to facilitate and plan effective meetings. I was learning and creating material on the run.

Opportunities appeared out of the blue, all in alignment with my mission. Over time, I gained a reputation for having something significant to say and having the ability to impact lives on both the personal and the professional fronts. I do have much to say, and I am not always aware of the source. I have been exposed to many brilliant teachers and influencers. I forget who said what at times, but I always attempt to give credit where credit is due. I also am attracting more and more original thoughts and ideas from a source that I believe is greater than me. The Universe, perhaps. I am able to incorporate these ideas into my work and message.

The audiences I attracted were influential leaders with considerable outreach. I kept getting better, more experienced, and more comfortable because my mission was pulling me along. I experienced what Nemerouf describes in this way: "The difference in performance between ordinary and extraordinary may be found in the clarity of focus, dedication to that focus, and the spirit brought to the pursuit." I had finally found it. Finally! I was clear, dedicated, and spirited.

That purpose resonates internally with me in all dimensions and has guided me on a daily basis in both my business life and my private life. I seldom, if ever, deviate from that purpose. This purpose is the defined filter that decides for me where I focus my work, interests, love, passion, resources, and energy. It serves me well. Abundance, joy, and gratitude follow at a level that I have never experienced in the past. I will ride this wave as long as it continues to create and attract positive results. When it no longer does, I will change it to be more in alignment with my internal transformation and the overall growth that I am experiencing.

FIND YOUR PURPOSE

Your purpose, either personal or professional, establishes your "red carpet" and keeps you between the velvet ropes and away from adoring and seductive distractions that reach out to you as you walk along that red carpet toward your vision. It allows you to resist the temptation of participating in immediate, self-gratifying short-term gains that can result in devastating long-term losses. It provides you with the momentum and focus to work through short-term losses for life-enhancing long-term gains.

As with most carpets, you can roll it up and unfurl it in another direction as your purpose changes through the different stages and cycles of your life. As you may have already discovered, life is not always totally predictable, no matter how much thoughtful intention you apply. Allow for a little wiggle room once you set something in motion. You are not laying down confining, nailed-in-place forms for a permanent concrete sidewalk.

Life is a series of intentional initiations and course corrections as we gain additional visibility of and new perspectives for the desired outcomes. Thomas à Kempis, Renaissance Roman Catholic monk and author of *The Imitation of Christ*, wrote that "Life without a purpose is a languid, drifting thing; every day we ought to review our purpose, saying to ourselves, 'This day let me make a sound beginning.'"

Make your sound beginning by defining your purpose. You are the only one who can determine where you are at this stage of your life, what legacy you will leave to others, and who will show up tomorrow as the latest and greatest version of you. If you own that accountability, you move toward becoming the person who fulfills the potential that lies within and attracts to you all of the treasures that the Universe has stacked on the shelves for you. If you do not own this stance in life, you may become a puppet that relies upon influences outside of you. Review from chapter 3 whether you are a low achiever or a high achiever. Do you seek an unremarkable or a remarkable life? Are you resigned to a life full of restrictions or have you designed a life full of expansions? Choose now. The clock is ticking.

I mentioned earlier that my purpose found me. However, once I had defined and positioned it in the Universe, it answered all of the criteria mentioned in the exercises that follow. Remember to keep your purpose simple, focused, and relevant to you. "As you simplify your life, the laws of the universe will be simpler; solitude will not be solitude, poverty will not be poverty, nor weakness be weakness," advised nineteenth-century American essayist, poet, and transcendentalist Henry David Thoreau. As I become older and hopefully wiser, I find I am moving more toward simplicity in all that I do. I am attempting to remove the clutter in my life and see things through a new and more enlightened filter. As Thoreau suggested, traditional thinking about solitude, poverty, and weakness may be cast in a different, more positive light as one simplifies and begins to understand how the greater natural laws of the Universe operate in bringing joy and fulfillment to people's lives.

Perhaps you can jump-start the process by answering the questions at the end of this chapter and broadcasting the answers to the ever-listening, receptive ears of the Universe as well as to the mechanisms of your brain.

EXERCISES

- When are you the happiest in your life and what are you doing?

- What are you the most passionate and inspired about in your life that appears sustainable?

- In what circumstances do you feel the best about yourself and others?

- When do you best exemplify your positive core values and under what circumstances and situations?

- What are you most fearful of achieving because it seems to be out of your reach yet won't go away from your thoughts, dreams, and desires? What are you daring yourself to do?

- What is the legacy that you want to leave behind and be known for?

- What path do you need to be on in order to reach your vision?

CHAPTER 8

CREATING MORE

Any person who selects a goal in life, which can be fully
achieved, has already defined his own limitations.

—CAVETT ROBERT
THE "DEAN OF PUBLIC SPEAKING"

Goals are the firm stepping-stones and benchmarks to your defined
vision. In order to reach your elevated, evolved vision, you must have
a ladder with well-constructed, firm, and supportive rungs. These are
your specific goals and accompanying robust actions. Make certain
you are leaning your ladder against the right wall—that is, *your* wall,
not someone else's.

Be courageous and define what you want and set your plan in
action. Do not let fear push you to settle for what others want for you,
or for what is familiar and knowingly within your reach. Here's how
actor Jack Nicholson puts it.

But the real fear I have to overcome, actually, is the fear of the unknown. We're very uncomfortable with the unknown, and that's why we tend to cling to the status quo, to structure, to relationships—to just cling. You start off today and every day by trying to overcome that fear with clarity. If you have clarity, it'll give you a position of power, the ability to act on your best instincts. Where there is clarity, there is no choice. Where there's choice, there's misery.

Choice can be a bit frightening because it involves being awake, making decisions, and then being accountable for your actions—and that can be scary and cause misery for many people.

Let's begin constructing your bucket list. You know all the things that you want to be, do, and have; all the things to start, stop, and continue, tangibly and intangibly, before you kick the bucket, or, as others say, buy the farm. Call that list the hundred things I aspire to experience before I die. Identify it as a series of things that are the non-negotiables in your life. Call it anything you want, but call it something, and start today and listen as it beckons to you.

Every day that you postpone, delay, or rationalize that this is not quite the right time, the right circumstance, or the exact and right place, you lose your place in line. That incessant clock just keeps on ticking, ticking, and ticking, not giving a hoot about you and your schedule.

Your custom-designed goals, in alignment with your vision, are what bring joy and gratitude to your heart, be it a new red Lamborghini, paying off your student loans, learning a second language, or contributing to an orphanage in a third world country. All four, and many others, are just fine, and you deserve to reach them and many more. It is *your* life, so go for whatever excites you, for what you feel passionate about. "Chance can allow you to accomplish a goal every once in a while, but consistent achievement happens only if you love what you are doing." That's good insight from Bart Conner, former Olympic gold medal gymnast and entrepreneur. What do you love to do?

If your life is a continual series of disappointments, missed opportunities, and failures, ask yourself why? After all, *you* are the only one who has been at the scene of every crime. So *you* need to be the lead investigator and examine your initial intentions and passions regarding the goals that you are manifesting or are missing.

CHECK OUT YOUR INTENTIONS

Your goals should hasten you along your way to your vision and be driven by powerful, thoroughly considered, and passionate intentions. Ask yourself the following questions as you determine your next set of outcomes:

1. What are my goals, and are they in consistent alignment with my vision?

2. What are the internal and external driving forces behind the goals that I am choosing?

3. Are my intentions honorable and consistent with my positive values?

4. Are my intentions going to positively and constructively benefit both others and me?

5. Will I transmit robust positive emotions out to the Universe because my intentions are pure, constructive, and coming from love, passion, joy, and gratitude?

Check out your motives for the goals you have set. If you suspect that you are out of alignment with your vision, have less than noble intentions, or are wishing for things that are contrary to your standards, put the car in reverse and correct your course. Keep the reverse gear well lubricated; you will need it if you expect to grow and evolve. Growth and evolution are seldom a straight-line journey to a steady and unmovable target.

Your intentions for your goals should bring you and others appropriate joy and gratitude. What you intend engages the appropriate gears and drives you toward the final experience—positive or negative. Remember that you are in a cause-and-effect model. The resulting outcome is the effect, and you control the cause by your intentional thoughts, words, mental pictures, and emotions.

EXPERIENCING YOUR DESIRED OUTCOMES

There are numerous templates for determining and experiencing your goals effectively. Here is mine, which works for me and may also work for you.

1. **You must have a desire or need for the goal.** Make certain that the result is well intended and links to your vision, as previously discussed. What this really means is that you cannot set goals for others unless they have a desire or need for the outcome. It is ill-advised to suggest to your loved one that it is your sincere desire for him or her to lose thirty pounds or get a facelift and liposuction procedure. Don't do it, or you will be sleeping with one eye open for a long time—if you are sleeping at home at all!

2. **Use the S-M-A-R-T method in setting your goals.** In 1954 Peter Drucker created the acronym SMART (specific, measurable, achievable, relevant, and time-bound) while discussing objective-based management in his book *The Practice of Management*. That acronym is a good template to use as you begin to set

your authentic and original goals. Let me explain each element of the S-M-A-R-T method in more detail.

(**S**) The written goal should be **specific**. That means no baffling ambiguity or confusing outcomes.

(**M**) The goal should be **measurable**. You can benchmark your progress to determine if you are on or off target.

(**A**) The goal should be **achievable**. Do not set yourself up for failure (like flying). Be reasonable. Do you have available or can you obtain the resources to reach the desired outcome?

(**R**) The goal should be **relevant** to you. You have a need, good intentions, and a passion for the outcome. It is your idea and desire.

(**T**) The goal should be **time-bound**. I believe that start dates, check-in points, and completion dates are important—include them as part of your process. Be aware, however, that such time targets can also create undo stress, pressure, and, often, procrastination.

Drucker's model can be expanded or constricted depending on who or what the goals are being applied to. A simpler model works well for individuals. A more sophisticated model can be used to set goals for corporations, involving more people, strategies, budgets, organization charts, and outside influences regarding economics, politics, geography, competition, bureaucracies, formal meetings, and so forth.

In chapter 5, I introduced you to my method of writing each category of my vision on an index card. On the backside of each of those vision cards I write my specific goals. Beneath each goal I then write my intention, that is, why I desire to achieve it. Here is the complete index card for my professional vision.

PROFESSIONAL VISION

I influence those who influence many. I am a world-class keynote speaker, corporate trainer, strategic-planning consultant, and a renowned published author. My partner and I are a team. I outsource appropriate tasks to keep the business simple. Advocates advise me and I accept their support and implement their ideas successfully. I attend seminars to improve my professional skills. I develop new material, products, and content, and remain highly visible. I am an articulate, humorous, passionate, engaged, present, entertaining, knowledgeable,

and stylish speaker. My presence, staging, audiovisuals, products, and content have an extraordinary impact. My writing is clear, concise, accurate, entertaining, thought provoking, and intelligent. I appear on talk shows and have positive articles and reviews from clients and the media.

PROFESSIONAL GOALS (BACKSIDE)

1. To book and deliver (specific number) or more keynotes annually at a minimum of (dollar figure) or greater per gig.

    The intention is to bring balance to my revenue stream.

2. To write and have published Aspire by March 2009.

    The intention is to influence people's lives and to further my writing career.

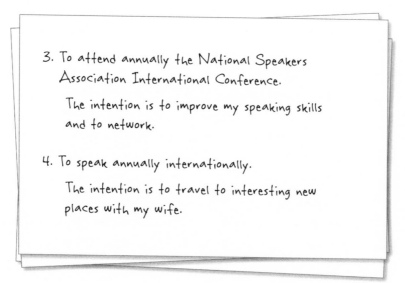

3. To attend annually the National Speakers Association International Conference.

    The intention is to improve my speaking skills and to network.

4. To speak annually internationally.

    The intention is to travel to interesting new places with my wife.

3. Convert each goal to a positive affirmation, visualize the end result of the goal, and launch the positive emotions. (I will show you how to do each of these steps in chapters 9, 10, and 11.) You will take specific actions to meet each goal. Taking action is essential, because if you do not, the energy will dissipate and the momentum will disappear.

At first glance this may seem like an overload of detail. It can be, but do not allow the process to overwhelm you. This is your beginner's starter kit, your training wheels. We are now walking and moving toward an eventual sprint to break the tape at the finish line. The process adds discipline and structure to get you started on the right path and going in the right direction. It allows you to develop new habits and to replace old—perhaps destructive—patterns that have not served you and others. Keep in mind that for many of you, this is an initiation into a new way of looking at your life; a little structure and order is necessary to launch your fresh beginnings. When asked how he got to be such a great musician, jazz saxophonist Charlie Parker responded: "You've got to learn your instrument. Then you practice, practice, practice. And then when you finally get up on the bandstand, forget all that and just wail." Go wail, but get the fundamentals in place first. Practice and practice and practice.

I believe that your vision, with its corresponding goals and intentions, is essentially put in motion when you declare it to the Universe. The remaining steps simply accelerate the pace at which you reach the desired goals and vision. You will find after a time that you are automatically affirming, visualizing, and broadcasting positive, powerful emotions relative to your specific goals and vision. If you are a beginner, go through all of the steps systematically. Keep in mind, practice does not make perfect. Perfect practice makes perfect. Do your best.

EXERCISES

- Write a goal that you desire regarding learning. Some examples could be to complete your MBA in the next three years, to read three books each month, or to subscribe to Soundview Executive Book Summaries (and read it!) for two years.

- Write a goal that you desire regarding health. Some examples could be to work out five days each week at the local gym, to reduce your body fat percentage to 12 percent, or to switch to eating only organic food.

- Write a goal that you desire regarding your spirituality. Some examples could be to read one spiritual book per month to learn about other forms of religion, to pray or meditate daily, or to tithe 10 percent of your income annually to a spiritual cause.

- Write a goal that you desire regarding something just for yourself. Some examples could be to buy a Harley-Davidson and ride it to Sturgis, South Dakota, to learn how to play golf by taking lessons from a PGA professional, or to take a class in abstract art.

- Write a goal that you desire regarding wealth. Some examples could be to earn $150,000 in 2009, to increase your net worth by 25 percent annually, or to make an appointment and create a plan with a financial adviser.

- Write a goal that you desire regarding relationships. Some examples could be to renew a loving, nurturing, and supportive relationship with your spouse, to meet a new friend once a month, or to make contact with an old friend each month.

STRATEGY 3:

THE MANIFESTATION TRILOGY

CHAPTER 9

THE TRILOGY: SAYING MORE

*Practice rather than preach. Make of your life an affirmation,
defined by your ideals, not the negation of others. Dare to the
level of your capability then go beyond to a higher level.*

—ALEXANDER HAIG
U.S. ARMY GENERAL AND FORMER SECRETARY OF STATE

Intentional, well-defined affirmations transform your goals and vision
into your desired reality. Through self-initiated and clearly identified
affirmations, you serve notice to the Universe and to your brain of what
you aspire to by linking your goals to deliberate, well-constructed, positive thoughts and spoken words. These robust thoughts and words
create powerful affirmations, goal-seeking magnets that attract to
you whatever it is you are affirming. "We need to understand that
thoughts are tools. Are we using them as productively as we can? Are
our thoughts serving us well, or are we their victims? It's up to us,"
says business speaker Dr. Tom Morris.

The affirmation process sets in motion the first step of the mani-festation trilogy: Saying More. Saying more is followed by step two, Seeing More—the visualization process—and by step three, Feeling More—the emotional component. Any thought or spoken words that follow "I am" is an affirmation, either positive or negative. "I am a winner" is an affirmation. "I am a loser" is an affirmation. Both posi-tive and negative affirmations set in motion the Law of Attraction and activate mechanisms of the brain with the same robust inten-sity. Your mind and the Universe do not censor the content or the intention of the affirmation. Both your mind and the Universe are designed to be and remain completely objective and nonjudgmental. It is your responsibility to stay conscious and intentional about what it is you are broadcasting to a powerful and responsive Universe. Consistent and persistent thoughts about what you aspire to be, do, and have are the magnets that attract the experience to you. "We cannot always control our thoughts, but we can control our words. And repetition impresses the subconscious, and we are then master of the situation," says Florence Scovel Shinn, American artist and author. Be your own master.

In chapter 1, when I was pointing out roadblocks you'll encounter in this process, I quoted Dr. Scott Peck, who said that "life is diffi-cult and people are lazy." These are not affirmations or declarations that I want you to embed permanently in your subconscious mind, influencing your core beliefs. It is not wise to internalize this message, broadcasting it out to the Universe, because you will attract more of life's self-imposed difficulties and pain-inflicting obstacles.

Life is difficult and people are lazy until you make those assertions untrue and stop affirming them as fact. Do not make those two state-ments absolute truths and part of your reality. You can determine and affirm any outcome by being conscious and intentional about your core beliefs, thoughts, spoken words, mental pictures, and emotions.

Affirmation—this recurrent conversation with yourself—continues whether or not you are aware of it. You will be successful with the manifestation process the more conscious and intentional you become regarding your internal dialogue and spoken words. Do not leave yourself vulnerable to intrusive and invasive thoughts that do not lead to your vision and goals, and that are not consistent with your core values. Do not be too concerned about the occasional negative thought or spoken word that passes through. You are not going to set the Law of Attraction in motion and activate automatic mechanisms of the mind unless there is continual robust focus and intention.

POSITIVE OR NEGATIVE SELF-TALK?

I assume that high and low achievers talk and think at the same rate of speed. If we could drop in on the thoughts and record the conversations of high achievers, we would find that the majority of the words and thoughts are positive, while low achievers' thoughts and conversations are largely negative. Thoughts and words create energy and frequencies that attract like energies and vibrations. We attract more of what we think and talk about, both positive and negative.

The results that you are experiencing in your life are your report card. They identify your dominant thoughts and spoken words. If the incoming is not what you want, change the outgoing frequencies one conscious thought, one deliberate word, at a time. Or shut down the broadcast, and be still. Follow the advice of Decimius Magnus Ausonius, a fourth-century Latin poet and rhetorician: "He who does not know how to be silent will not know how to speak." Silence can do the heavy lifting. You can use the power of silence if you remain aware and monitor what it is you are hearing, what you are about to say, and what you are thinking. This process requires that you be intentional about what you are saying to yourself and others. You are in control of most circumstances of your life and certainly your responses to them. Or have you given that responsibility to others?

Now I'd like to show you one more level I've added to what's written on my professional vision index card. Earlier you saw the specific goals and intentions I had written on the back of the card. I also record an affirmation for each goal. The following card can serve as an example of how to write correctly, in form and content, corresponding affirmations. Remember, though, this is how I prefer to do it. You do what works best for you.

PROFESSIONAL GOALS (BACKSIDE)

1. To book and deliver (specific number) or more keynotes annually at a minimum of (dollar figure) or greater per gig.

   The intention is to bring balance to my revenue stream.

   Affirmation: With joy and gratitude I book (#) or more keynotes annually @ ($) or more per gig.

2. To write and have published Aspire by March 2009.

   The intention is to influence people's lives and to further my writing career.

   Affirmation: Aspire is written, published, and continually influences people in a positive manner.

3. To attend annually the National Speakers Association International Conference.

   The intention is to improve my speaking skills and to network.

   Affirmation: I thoroughly enjoy attending and learning @ the annual NSA conference and networking with other professional speakers.

4. To speak annually internationally.

The intention is to travel to interesting new places with my wife.

Affirmation: I travel annually to new and exciting international locations for speaking engagements and to enjoy time with my wife.

EXERCISES

- On the backside of each of your 5 × 7 "vision statement" index cards, craft the affirmations that correspond to each goal and intention. Remember to write them in the "PPP" style: personal (pronoun), positive (direction toward the goal), and present tense (verb). Embellish the affirmations with words that excite you and engage your emotions. Use words that help you see yourself experiencing the goal. Practice until you are satisfied that each affirmation captures the goal and intention and broadcasts to the Universe exactly what you want to see occur. Experiment.

- Find a time of day when you are relaxed, uninterrupted, and free of duties, and begin affirming by reading your affirmations aloud. Read them with gusto and passion. Your aim here is to co-engage the Law of Attraction with the mechanistic capabilities of your brain. Let those partners know what you want in an intentional, joyous, and grateful manner. Watch for positive results, and take action when "inklings" become evident. Keep it simple. You are on your way.

CHAPTER 10

THE TRILOGY: SEEING MORE

Visualization is daydreaming with a purpose.

—BO BENNETT
BUSINESSMAN, PROGRAMMER, DESIGNER,
MARTIAL ARTIST, AND MOTIVATIONAL SPEAKER

Your vision, goals, intentions, and affirmations will generate explicit pictures of the end result of what it is that you are affirming. When you are able to see yourself having what you say is important to you and are able to bring this picture into your awareness with crystal clarity, you are one step closer to having what you desire. You have the power to visualize what you want instead of nonchalantly, unconsciously, and innocently accepting what you have.

Many people have a difficult time affirming what it is that they aspire to because they cannot see themselves having it. But your mind's eye has unlimited potential; it has no limitations. True imagination accepts no constraints if you turn it loose, childlike, uninhibited, and unencumbered by destructive and limiting messages of your past.

Think about what you are able to create in your dreams while sleeping. There are no limitations. Nothing seems impossible. You are able to perform and be in situations that, from the perspective of the Earth's expanse, are impossible. People pop into your life, making cameo appearances; you perform Herculean feats; events change without advance notice; and emotions are aroused at an unbelievable level. You are multidimensional to the max. Nothing is beyond your reach.

Remember as a youngster how, with your vivid imagination, you could be anyone, do anything, go anywhere—just like the characters in the movies you watched or the stories and comic books you read? You could make it all real with few inhibitions. I want you to return to those days. Your imagination is the ultimate explorer and creator.

As a child, I did not have a television. The radio was my primary source of entertainment, and it stimulated my imagination. I grew up listening to the Green Hornet, Flash Gordon, the Shadow, Amos and Andy, the Jack Benny Show, the Cisco Kid, Roy Rogers, George Burns and Gracie Allen, Red Rider, Edgar Bergen with Charlie McCarthy and Mortimer Snerd, the Red Skelton show, and Fibber McGee and Molly, among others. I had no idea what any of the characters looked like, but I imagined their appearance and reenacted my version of the programs and scripts following the radio broadcasts. Author Peter Nivio Zarlenga believes that your thoughts have the ability "to see what the eyes cannot see . . . to hear what the ears cannot hear . . . and to feel what the heart cannot feel." Many have lost that capability and opportunity in today's highly technical multimedia world. For many of us, what we need to do for ourselves is being done for us by others.

Golf legend Jack Nicklaus said that he visualized every shot before striking the ball. According to golf-teaching professional Jim Flick:

"For all truly great athletes, the eyes are productive and profound. Jack's eyes missed nothing! The information and pictures they sent to his brain created a marvelous sensation. His eyes committed his mind and body to the target, so his hands and arms felt and swung the club in sync with his feet and legs. The state of a completely focused mind is a trademark of a champion."

I have observed that many great champions and leaders, no matter what their field—sports, business, the arts—have the ability to mentally rehearse with guided imagery what it is they are attempting to accomplish. In their mind's eye, they always succeed, coming close to perfection. They transform the impossible into the possible, the unobtainable into the obtainable, and daydreams into everyday, commonplace reality. Motivation expert Dr. Denis Waitley explains it this way:

> I took the visualizations process from the Apollo program, and instituted it during the 1980s and '90s into the Olympic program. It was called Visual Motor Rehearsal. When you visualize then you materialize . . . We took Olympic athletes and had them run their events only in their mind, and then hooked them to sophisticated biofeedback equipment . . . The same muscles fired in the same sequence when they were running the race in their mind as when they were running it on the track. How could this be? Because the mind can't distinguish whether you are doing it or whether it is just a practice. If you go there in your mind, you'll go there in [your] body.

When you think about and visualize desired outcomes, you are not bound by confining borders, sacred cows, or that which has been your past reality. If you want your life to be larger, you need to first see yourself in a vast existence, rich with loving relationships, unlimited abundance, perfect health, and fulfilled dreams. This part you can control and design. It is your storyboard, your screenplay, your goal poster, and your animated cartoon. You can create results that are healthy and sound, without problems, inhibitors, or limitations. You need to be intentional about this exercise. It takes focus to establish new habits. Would you rather take a little bit of time to develop new habits or settle for what you have created in the past?

Your thoughts are free to explore possibilities and create blueprints of the next moment that will bring you joy, gratitude, and unbridled fulfillment. Let your imagination propel you to your vision, to your open-ended potential. Sweep aside those self-limiting beliefs that have thrown tacks in the road on your journey to happiness and fulfillment. You have the power and the mechanisms to separate yourself from the limitations of others and remain invested entirely on what is possible for you. Stay awake and focus on what you desire, not the unsatisfactory that drains your passion for the life that you aspire to have.

POSITIVE OR NEGATIVE PICTURES?

Our thoughts trigger internal pictures. These positive or negative images of what we are thinking about manifest external realities—the home movies and still pictures of our lives. We see ourselves at some future point in time possessing a new car, being in a close relationship that benefits us, up on stage performing spectacularly, or reaching a desired outcome of more money in the bank. Or not.

With consistency and focus on such details as color, motion, and sound, we move toward our mental pictures, both positive and negative, with accelerating speed until our momentum carries us to the end. Our initial, perhaps crude, creative storyboard becomes a full-blown dynamic episode in our life's long-running movie that is archived into our subconscious. In *Think and Grow Rich*, Napoleon Hill states, "Whatever the mind of man can conceive and believe, it can achieve."

This process works both ways, though. If you are creating mental pictures of negative results, then that is what you are going to experience. And you'll experience those negative results with the same energy and velocity with which positive results have entered your life. If the story of your life has not been what you want, then you need to project a new, more positive image to the Universe, starting with positive affirmations that you support with vivid mental pictures of the results you want. Don't forget: The mind can achieve whatever it can conceive. Can you conceive of yourself reversing what is not working in your life and constructing a future that brings you joy? If you can, then start now. Create a picture of your life that you aspire to. If you cannot, then you will remain stuck in the role that you let others assign to you. The good news is that you are the one in control if you will just take responsibility for your life.

GUIDELINES FOR VISUALIZING WHAT YOU WANT

Let's keep this simple. I have outlined the fundamental steps of effective visualization. The key is to focus on the end result of the goal with as much vividness and realism as possible.

1. **Picture in your mind's eye the obtainment of the vision, goal, or desired outcome.** Visualize the outcome of the goal, not the process and the multitude of individual actions required to reach it. That methodology and process will come to you the clearer you are about the end result. The road could get a bit crooked, and there are critical decision points and forks along the journey. If the picture is fuzzy, the result will reflect that and add more confusion and ambiguity.

If you have difficulty visualizing with exact clarity, think about the end result of the goal in extreme detail. Reflect upon every aspect of the outcome, not the process. Some people see a blank screen when they close their eyes and they become frustrated and give up.

I am fortunate because I am a visual learner. I think consistently in pictures. But there are many other ways to get to where you want to go. Do not limit the how, the path, and the strategy. You will discover the way that works best for you. I will provide you with one way. You have internal mechanisms that will make the appropriate corrections for you as you proceed on your journey. As a human being who is teleological in nature, you will automatically make the corrections necessary to reach your goal.

Your eyes are the lenses of the camera focusing on the outcome of what you want to achieve. You are not taking a still-framed picture or filming an action movie of yourself from an external position; rather, you are recording what you want from an internal perspective. You are the camera, and the film is inside your head recording the finished product. You are also the screenwriter, director, cameraperson, editor, investor, producer, animator, key-grip, and eventual recipient of the golden Oscar that accompanies the accomplishment.

I mentioned earlier in this chapter that Jack Nicklaus saw in his mind's eye where he wanted the golf ball to land—*that* was his target, not his swing. "I never hit a shot, not even in practice, without having a very sharp, in-focus picture of it in my head. It's like a color movie." The movie followed the flight and shape of the ball after it left his clubhead to where he wanted the ball to land, in the fairway, on the green, or in the cup. The technique and the muscle memory required to send the ball on that trajectory to create that end result all adjusted to the movie in his mind. He had his internal storyboard in place before he actually hit the next shot. Nicklaus believed that his considerable success was a result of 10 percent technique, 40 percent position, and 50 percent visualization—the mental picturing of a successful shot for each situation.

Picture your outcomes in vivid detail, but omit all of the implementation steps from your visualization. See your monthly bank statement, your yearly income tax return, or your check stub reflecting abundance and wealth—not the method or hard work that went into creating the remarkable numbers. Visualize yourself opening the front door of the house you deserve and aspire to have—not the tedious buying-a-home steps of saving, searching, inspecting, and negotiating. See the relationship you yearn for as an exchange of wedding rings or that fitness goal as the finish line with you completing the marathon. Send these vivid pictures of success to your subconscious mind; your mind will actualize them and use them to attract more of the same. Let go and trust the process.

If you have a high need to control most everything in your life, effective visualization might prove to be a difficult task. Trust, faith, and confidence are essential in this process. Letting go of the exact *how* and focusing on and emphasizing the *outcome* is the technique that I am suggesting. You need to believe that whatever you want, within reason, is on its way.

I like the way William James, the father of American psychology, expressed this belief: "The greatest discovery of the nineteenth century was not in the realm of the physical sciences, but the power of the subconscious mind touched by faith. Any individual can tap into an eternal reservoir of power that will enable them to overcome any problem that may arise. All weaknesses can be overcome, bodily healing, financial independence, spiritual awakening, and prosperity beyond your wildest dreams. This is the superstructure of happiness." Start by creating your pictures of achievement.

2. **Your subconscious mind does not differentiate between an actual event and one that is imagined vividly.** Once the mental picture

is clearly in place, you will start acting, behaving, and thinking as if you already have what you are visualizing. Emotions will be consistent with the visualization. When you see yourself closing the sale, making the shot, or paying off the loan, emotions that are consistent with the imagined event will fill you and erupt from you. You will broadcast confidence, joy, gratitude, satisfaction, excitement, and other feelings that reflect you reaching the desired goal.

Make certain that you bring as much detail and vibrancy to your mental pictures as possible because they will seem real to your subconscious mind. You may have experienced this process when you found yourself daydreaming, worrying, or recalling a past positive or negative event and literally moved your emotions to anxiety, tears, or outright laughter. You have created a reality in your mind's eye that your powerful subconscious thinks is occurring. Do not leave this process to chance. You are intentionally creating vivid pictures of your desired outcomes, not casual or undisciplined daydreams.

Remember to focus on what you want, not what you are attempting to avoid. It works both ways: You can load positive or negative pictures into your subconscious, and your subconscious won't know the difference. It won't give off any warning signals before manifestation gains significant traction and reaches out to the Universe for completion. "Our subconscious minds have no sense of humor, play no jokes, and cannot tell the difference between reality and an imagined thought or image. What we continually think about eventually will manifest in our lives," wrote Robert Collier, a twentieth-century American self-help author.

3. **Consistently visualize the end result of the goal when you are relaxed and uninterrupted.** I want you to keep this process simple. You do not have to assume the (to me, very uncomfortable) lotus position with palms upward and chakras perfectly aligned, chant mantras, or go into a deep meditative state. You just need to be someplace

where you can relax and be undistracted and uninterrupted. In other words, visualization won't work while you're sitting at some busy metropolitan intersection waiting for the light to turn green.

Songwriter Johnny Nash wrote in the early 1970s about visualizing and the emotions that accompanied his picture of what he wanted his future to be in his hit song "I Can See Clearly Now." His song is full of hope, truthfulness, optimism, affirmations, vision, and clarity. The lyrics showed he is committed to a better tomorrow and no longer in denial about his past. What is your song for your future?

Visualization is the second step in the manifestation trilogy. It is an essential component that, with practice, you will become more effective doing. It works best when there is clarity about your goal, which triggers explicitness regarding what you are visualizing. The exercises on the next page will assist you in becoming better at visualization.

EXERCISES

Here are three visualization exercises that will demonstrate the power of visualization and guided imagery. Have a partner read them aloud to you. Go slowly and follow the directions of each exercise. Repeat them often to sharpen your skills. You will be amazed at the results.

The Rose: This exercise increases your attention to detail and will help you notice and embellish that which you are focusing upon. It allows you to bring forth many of your senses so that the picture in your mind sends a strong signal to your subconscious.

Place yourself in a relaxed position where there are no external distractions. Close your eyes and take several deep breaths until you feel your body is relaxed and your mind is clear of any thoughts.

In your mind's eye picture a beautiful single red rose. See its stem and several green leaves in a clear, narrow, elegant glass vase. The vase is on a small wooden stand. Notice the shape of the petals of the rose, their vibrant red color contrasted against the green of the leaves and the stem. See the drops of moisture that are slowly sliding off the petals and dripping down the stem and leaves.

Now focus on the stem and the thorns. Notice the color, shape, and length of the stem and thorns. Move your eye to the vase; notice where the water level is and the clarity of the water nourishing the rose.

Lift the vase from the wooden stand and bring the rose close to your face. Examine the rose from this perspective and begin to let the wonderful familiar fragrance of the rose enter into your awareness. With your right hand gently pick the rose

EXERCISES (CONTINUED)

from the vase and feel it. Softly and gently twirl the rose in your hand. Notice the cool, moist, soft texture of the petals and feel the firmness of the stem. Allow all of your senses to fully experience this wonder of nature.

When you are ready, gently place the rose into the vase and take in the entire scene, permitting whatever emotions you may feel to enter into your awareness.

The Arm: This exercise demonstrates how potential can be unleashed as you imagine yourself going beyond your normal self-imposed limitations.

With your eyes open, stand still and straight in the middle of a spacious room. Roll your shoulders back and place your arms at your side. Plant your feet squarely on the floor, shoulder width apart, and distribute your weight evenly on each foot.

Facing straight ahead, extend your right arm from your shoulder straight out in front of you at a right angle to your body and parallel to the floor. Make a fist with your right hand, with your right thumb pointing up. Pretend that your right arm is a rifle and your thumb is the gunsight at the end of the barrel.

Now, with your feet still firmly planted on the floor, turn your body to the right, leading with your right arm. Swivel at the waist and fix your eye on your raised right thumb (the gunsight) until you reach resistance. Try to go further until you cannot without losing your footing. Look down the barrel of your right arm, through the raised thumb (gunsight), and shoot a hole in the wall opposite the sight. Notice exactly where that bullet hole is on the wall.

EXERCISES (CONTINUED)

Now swivel back to your original position and close your eyes. In your mind's eye (that is, with your eyes closed and your body still—don't actually move) repeat the exercise, only this time see the gunsight going well past the point in the wall where you fired the first shot.

Open your eyes and repeat the original exercise. Shoot a new hole in the wall, way past the previous hole. How far did you go past the first hole in the wall? One yard, three yards, ten yards, more? That is the power of visualization releasing the potential within you.

The Lemon: This exercise illustrates how your body may respond to mental pictures that trick your subconscious into believing the pictures are reality. You will begin to behave differently, as if what you are picturing is in your actual possession.

Close your eyes and picture in your mind's eye a fresh, chilled lemon. Notice the oval shape and bright yellow color of the lemon. Feel the texture of the outer skin. Be aware of the scent of the lemon, its size, weight, and anything else that might catch your attention.

Picture placing the lemon on a wooden cutting board, holding it firmly with your fingers and pressing it against the surface of the board. With your other hand, take a sharp kitchen knife and slice through the middle of the lemon until it falls away in two even pieces on either side of the blade.

EXERCISES (CONTINUED)

Put the knife down on the cutting board and pick up one of the halves. Bring it up to your nose and inhale the aroma. Squeeze the lemon until lemon juice begins to drip. Now take the lemon and bring it up to your mouth. Sink your teeth into the fruit and squeeze the juice into your mouth. Notice anything happening? Perhaps your mouth puckers slightly? Or does your mouth feel just a little dry?

As you experience these responses to an imagined event, you realize that the subconscious mind believes that the lemon is real and thus creates the auto-response.

CHAPTER 11

THE TRILOGY: FEELING MORE

When we direct our thoughts properly, we can control our emotions.

—W. CLEMENT STONE
BUSINESSMAN, PHILANTHROPIST, AND AUTHOR OF SELF-HELP BOOKS

Your vision and supporting goals give birth to specific affirmations. Your spoken word and inner dialogue create mental pictures. The mental pictures trigger and create powerful positive emotions. These vigorous and robust emotions are imprinted into and stored permanently in your subconscious mind while they simultaneously broadcast a penetrating frequency into a vast and responsive Universe. You attract to you whatever it is you are visualizing and emoting about. An internal-external engagement has occurred, and you initiated the union. And you thought you were just having some casual thoughts, visions, and feelings. Think again. You are much more powerful than you imagined.

External to you, like attracts like, and a match is made in a responsive and objective Universe. A door is opened and a bond is formed with whatever goals you set, affirm, picture, and feel positive or negative about. That bond is waiting for you on the other side of the threshold. All three steps of the manifestation trilogy are deliberate. The emotion that you feel will be in direct relationship to the meaningfulness of the goal that you are affirming, the thoughts that you are thinking, and the implicitness of the visualization. You must experiment with the affirmation and the visualization until they create a favorable emotion that brings you joy, gratitude, and fulfillment.

Stay conscious. It is up to you to focus on what you want more of and how you are going to feel about those results. The process works both for and against you, with equal power. Be careful what you wish for because you just might get it. "You can have anything you want if you want it desperately enough. You must want it with an inner exuberance that erupts through the skin and joins the energy that created the world," says Sheila Graham, former actor and famous Hollywood gossip columnist. I agree with Sheila, as long as you keep the "desperation" need in proper context. I prefer that you come from a position of aspiration and desire, not frenzied need and absurd ego-influenced and anxiety-filled wants.

It is your choice to influence and define the feelings that are most beneficial to you in this creative process. You possess the power to do this. If the picture you are holding in your consciousness does not introduce exciting, positive, and constructive emotions and feelings, then recast the visualization until you feel the change. The emotion should be positive and pleasurable so that you will want the affirmation and visualization.

Rewrite your storyboard. Make corrections to your script. The keyboard and camera are both ready to be instruments in your capable hands. You may have to embellish the picture with bright colors, exciting action, amplified sounds, or whatever it takes to entice you into feeling more positive and passionate. Keep experimenting until it feels more appropriate to the situation. Whatever emotions you are feeling will perpetuate additional thoughts, pictures, and powerful follow-on emotions that create either a productive or an unproductive cycle.

POSITIVE OR NEGATIVE EMOTIONS?

People will argue that they can't help how they feel, that certain feelings overwhelm them under certain conditions, such as when they hear a specific song, see a remarkable sunset, or participate in a wedding. Emotions are never killed off; they get buried alive in our subconscious mind. They tend to show up in situations that are similar to the original imprint.

I believe that we can significantly influence how we feel and what we emote in most situations, even overriding the original imprint. This requires that we remain conscious and aware, and that we choose. Our thoughts, words, and mental pictures spawn our emotions and feelings. Our emotions then create new thoughts and pictures, which further creates a cycle of new or reinforced emotions. It is how we hold a situation based upon our past experiences that determines the flow of our feelings and emotions and how we consciously influence the cycle.

Emotions are powerful and penetrating. We all know that since we experience them daily. They leak, drip, drain, and flow from us in the form of tears. They erupt from us when least expected in fits of spontaneous laughter and joy or of irritation and anger. They are capable of casting us to bottomless dark pits of despair and sorrow and bitterness. Sometimes we just go numb because we don't want to feel. The effects of emotions seem endless.

At times emotions fill us to the brim at opposite polarities of exhilaration and agitation. We attempt to choke them back, or we allow them to cascade from us with naive abandonment, hoping for revelation, insight, and self-discovery in the presence of a trusted therapist. They gush over us, fill us, overcome us, reduce us, and render us limp and exhausted.

Psychopaths are said to be void of emotion as they contemplate or implement unthinkable, despicable, Hannibal Lector–inspired acts. Men claim that women have far too many emotions, labeling the *weaker* sex illogical, out of control, and confused. Women want and expect men to express more emotion and to get in touch with their feelings. Men question the sexual orientation of other men who exhibit what are considered inappropriate emotions in certain circles. We are scolded and warned that there is no place for emotions in business, battle, or serious problem solving.

Emotions and feelings are confusing, yet they are totally essential to the manifestation process. When positive, robust emotions are linked with positive thoughts, words, and pictures, a powerful, penetrating three-pronged frequency is transmitted throughout the Universe, seeking and attracting like frequencies. At some point, matching occurs, engaging, securing, and capturing the goal. All of this is a natural process of the human experience and the Universe. This manifestation trilogy can be deliberate, intentional, and conscious, with you at the control panel pulling the levers and pushing the buttons. Get in the driver's seat and buckle up.

You can create a remarkable life. You are able to determine what comes your way and influence how you are going to feel about your life and the circumstances that you create and encounter. The other alternative is to take your chances and let life happen to you, to experience the emotions and feelings that accompany the undeclared circumstances. Like the advertisers tell us, life comes at you fast.

Victimhood, martyrdom, and subordination possibly await you. It is up to you and the choices you make, moment-by-moment, day-by-day, to make your life remarkable and to be in complete alignment with what you aspire to have more of.

DEALING WITH NEGATIVE EMOTIONS AND FEELINGS

I often hear people moan about certain events that have happened in their lives; how those events were unfair and unwarranted. They may be right. Those negative events probably should not have occurred, but they did, and at some significant or unconscious level, the moaners participated in creating the result. Now they are stuck with it.

When something you feel is unjust happens to you, nobody will care more than you do, because others are more concerned about their own stuff. But if you do not assume a stance of accountability in your life, it will be difficult for you to alter uninvited effects. An event that you feel should not have happened might trigger uninvited emotions and feelings of disappointment, frustration, sadness, and anger that will not serve you well. You will most likely set in motion the downward spiral of additional negative thoughts, mental pictures, and emotions. Down and down you will go, accelerating to more unproductive and unconstructive emotions and negative thoughts. Be accountable. How could you justify any other position?

Getting Over It—or Not

I continually advise people faced with adversity to do whatever it takes to get over it, whatever "it" is. I say this with an open and loving heart to encourage them to move on at the appropriate speed and not be held hostage by negative thinking, old embedded tapes and programs of the past. I want you to be looking forward to what you aspire to, not back at what you did not want to experience. I need to scale back this philosophy somewhat, however, as it is not an appropriate strategy in all situations.

Sometimes the natural process of healing—grieving the loss of a loved one, for example, or experiencing the subsequent emotional hurt of being rejected by someone that you care deeply about—is just not as easy as simply "getting over it." Getting over it may be contrary to what is needed in those situations. It could be a disservice to you and others.

Let me give you a personal example. I was having a conversation with one of my daughters, Heather. I was discussing a separation that I was experiencing with two people whom I love dearly. I said to her with conviction, "I just need to get over it and move on to something more positive. I can't let this situation define me any longer. It's too painful and unproductive."

From her twenty-something perspective, Heather replied, "Look Dad, I don't think that you should just get over it."

"Why not?" I interrupted. "I teach other people to do it. It would be hypocritical on my part to exclude myself."

"I know that this is devastating to you and dominates your thoughts and moods," she said. "You're grieving a loss that deserves something more than just getting over it."

"Like what?" I asked, leaning in so I could hear her answer.

"Well, like doing the right thing instead of doing things right. You taught me that not all situations are equal. Remember, one shoe doesn't fit all?"

"So Heather, what's the right thing to do?"

"The right thing to do is to give yourself a break and let your feelings run their course. If you were complaining about a break-in of your car, I would be on your get-over-it wagon. But not on this one—no way. Any more questions?"

"Nope."

Heather is right: Getting over it is not a one-shoe-fits-all strategy that applies to every situation. It can be harsh, intrusive, bold, and totally inappropriate to try to just get over an experience or emotion. Still, the choice is yours to do so, eventually, given the appropriate circumstances. You have the ability to create and respond to your life in any manner that you choose, and to get past being stuck. After getting advice from my daughter, I worked on the situation from an entirely different and fresh perspective. I allowed myself a little breathing room, with good intention and a loving open heart. The progress seemed snail slow, but I was hopeful and stayed with it.

Do not allow your immediate gut reactions to situations dominate. You might need time to heal and to move through a series of emotional stages. Be aware of the sequence that people consistently pass through when experiencing substantial loss, such as the death of a loved one or the news of a terminal illness. The stages that have been identified are feelings of shock or disbelief, denial, anger, depression, bargaining, guilt, and acceptance and hope.

These emotions do not apply to every situation, especially when one experiences adversity or tangible setbacks. How you respond to what life throws you is situational.

HOW I LEARNED ABOUT APPROPRIATE EMOTIONS—THE HARD WAY

On a less significant scale, I learned this lesson of appropriate emotions and perspective in an abrupt and memorable way. It left a lasting impression on how I went about my life. Amnesia sets in occasionally, but I now do what I need to do to stay conscious.

In 1983, I had been hired by a reputable and popular Northwest training company as a contractor to teach goal-setting and self-esteem seminars. The material fell under the umbrella of the psychology of self-esteem and was time-tested curriculum. It was a subject that I needed to be attentive to and apply to my life in order to move forward. I was ready and overjoyed with the opportunity and approached the assignment with a newly discovered passion and enthusiasm. I was finally engaged with my purpose.

The director of training passed me over continually in the schedule, favoring the well-known and familiar facilitators he had hired. I was not included in that group because at that time I was perceived as having "light" academic credentials and limited experience in the field that we were teaching. He had a point that made sense to him and his colleagues. He and they had advanced degrees in psychology and I was a walk-on from the streets hired by the CEO/owner of the company. I was viewed as an outsider and not an equal.

The director thought the CEO's decision to hire me was intrusive and disrespectful of his own position and authority. Continuing to come up short in the rotation, I decided to go over his head and meet with the CEO to resolve my concerns. He was my advocate, after all, and I was getting nowhere with the current strategy. I believe that you should try something different if what you are doing is getting zero results.

The CEO was a high roller and powerful leader involved in multiple publicly traded companies. He was the kind of guy who carries a roll of hundred-dollar bills held together with a rubber band in his pocket at all times. He granted me an appointment because he had invested in me and given me the original opportunity. I explained my position. He listened respectfully, with interest, and immediately corrected the situation by making a couple of telephone calls in my presence, thus satisfying my request for more activity. He placed me in the schedule and put the director of training on notice to mix up the rotation to provide more opportunities for me.

I thought at last I was getting somewhere and receiving the respect that I desired and deserved. Exhilaration drove me forward to continue the conversation. Not really conscious of what I was doing, right then and there I pushed for more assignments, perks, and input into the curriculum. My emotions went from joyfulness and gratefulness to forcefulness and aggressiveness. I was on a roll, oblivious to what was going on. I was going to get my just desserts by seizing the moment.

I quickly learned, however, that the Universe has this unique ability to put one on notice without much warning. Unbeknownst to me, a match was being made in the Universe of like frequencies. It happened in an instant. The CEO's negativity came out, guns blazing.

"Carlson, I don't owe you a thing," the CEO said angrily, glaring at me over his aircraft carrier–size desk. "I just took appropriate and considerate care of your problem. Right? That's what you came here for. Am I right? Do you hear me? Are you listening? I am extremely busy and have more important things to do than listen to your ungratefulness and exaggerated complaints. This meeting is over. It's over. There's the door."

I don't know if you have ever been in a situation similar to that, but if you have, like me you knew it was inappropriate to further the negotiation. You also knew your best move was to quietly and gracefully exit the room as humbly as possible. I chose that strategy.

A wave of humiliation and embarrassment rapidly cascaded over me. *The CEO's right*, I thought. Isn't it interesting how my emotions shifted so quickly from being aggressive, righteous, and confident to being down and beaten? It happened in a New York minute. I had failed to acknowledge his contribution with joy and gratitude. I got lost in my own emotional indignation and forgot my original intention of getting positioned in the facilitation queue. I had allowed the moment to define me instead of me defining the moment with a more positive response. The end result was that I became separated from my "gift."

It was a difficult but an essential lesson to learn. I wound up leaving the CEO's spacious office with my head down, offering a feeble apology and a mumbled thank-you, and saying good-bye. It was a long walk out of that office to my car. I have always respected and remembered that valuable lesson. I was chagrined, humiliated, and dumb wrong!

FREE YOURSELF FROM SELF-INFLICTED PAIN

These occasional setbacks in life are the spawning ground for negative feelings that are often launched automatically and instantly because we have conditioned ourselves to respond in a certain manner, under certain conditions. When things are not going your way and negative emotions erupt, make a deliberate shift and get interested intentionally in feeling better, being more positive, and acting more appropriately. You can do this if you remain alert. Make this your new focus. It might take considerable conscious and purposeful effort on your part, but why participate any longer in the train wreck?

The template is in place. You invented it and are the source of energy that perpetuates or changes it. You are ultimately the one in control and accountable. Do not get trapped in the justification of "Oh, that's what I always do in these situations." It may be what you used to do, but now, in this moment, multiple responses are at your beck and call if you stay awake and are aware. Always come up with another option in a challenging situation. Do not let the past dictate your open-ended potential, the life that is waiting to be created by you.

What follows is a list of productive steps you can use to free yourself from your self-inflicted pain:

1. **Your braking mechanism starts with your awareness that the negative feelings are either clutching you already or on their way.** You will feel the signals. Like Tony Robbins, I believe that success as well as failure leaves clues. Stay aware. Without awareness, you are bound hopelessly to your conditioned past.

2. **In order to break this unproductive pattern, inhale deeply and become centered by continual deep breathing.** It is that simple. Pull the fresh oxygen deep down into the depths of your lungs. Fill your lungs fully as you draw the air into the far-reaching borders of your lungs. Imagine a balloon being blown up to the point of almost exploding. Feel the pressure in your lower diaphragm as you press against your belt or waistline with each breath.

3. **Remain still and let silence do the heavy lifting to stop the momentum.** It may seem like a long and uncomfortable time, but you need to throw out the anchor to halt the descent into triggered, nonproductive reactions. It only seems slow; in reality, it will be just a matter of seconds. Ask yourself a question that shifts you toward a cognitive and productive state of awareness and problem solving. For instance: "I wonder why I am feeling this way right now? What conditions brought this on? Where have I experienced this before? How can I respond differently?" In answering these or similar questions, you will begin to seek resolution and allow yourself the opportunity to choose a different response. It is a deliberate movement of consciousness from the amygdala (old brain) to the neocortex (new brain). Keep

focused on resolution and loosening the grip of the bad feelings.

4. **Recast the situation by creating a fresh, more positive picture in your mind of the immediate circumstances.** Reach back into your memory bank and vividly picture a time when you were responding to situations in a more constructive manner. Let those feelings seep into your consciousness and gain dominance. See yourself responding differently from how you have in the past under similar situations.

5. **Affirm that you are in control with personal and positive sentences in the present tense.** "I am in control of my feelings and am feeling better with each breath." Keep repeating this, or a similar affirmation, until you notice the change in your emotions and are in control of your thoughts. If you are skeptical of these techniques, do some soul searching. It suggests that you are more invested in remaining where you are instead of experimenting and interrupting the pattern. It is your choice.

6. **Open the gate and allow more positive emotions to enter.** You are not denying your true feelings; you are simply making a better choice for yourself so that you do not become stuck or perpetuate the situation and give it additional shelf life.

This process requires focus, but the end result is more satisfying than the familiar auto-response that will only weaken you. It is essential that you make a conscious effort to alter the descending emotions by any means that work for you. Try the previous outlined steps next time you feel yourself being captured by immediate unwanted and destructive emotions. It really is up to you.

Nobody can make you feel anything. I will say that again in case you missed it. *Nobody can make you feel anything.* You have control over your responses. Choose wisely or become a victim. I know that this is a difficult choice, and it requires awareness and courage. Your ego and your fears will be screaming at you that life is unfair, and together your ego and fears will be scanning the immediate horizon for someone or something to blame. Break the cycle by taking a deep breath and considering with an uncluttered mind the consequences of continuing the conditioned responses you have automatically reacted with in the past. Consider the other choices and step into them. Yes, it might seem scary, unfamiliar, and nerve-wracking, with no guarantees, but what if making a different choice corrects the course of your life? Wouldn't that be worth the risk? Think about it for a short time and make a decision that may change your life forever. I wish you well.

THINGS ARE NEVER AS GOOD OR AS BAD AS THEY MIGHT SEEM IF YOU LIVE BETWEEN THE PLUS AND MINUS TENS

Do not become a slave to circumstances just because changes in those circumstances might require significant exertion on your part, an abrupt and sudden left turn, or even a complete about-face from what you do habitually. Be in charge of your internal experience regardless of your external environment. Otherwise, you become a dummy held hostage to the whims of the ventriloquist holding you on his or her lap and controlling all the moves.

Some suggest that all events are neutral. If I were to measure any event in my life on a scale of zero to ten, the actual occurrence would be a zero, neither positive nor negative, as the following diagram suggests. This will be a stretch for many of you, so please stay engaged. The view of the person coming into the event determines the event's energy. It can be positive or negative, happy or sad, safe or dangerous, and on and on. People bring their own luggage with them anywhere they go and thus influence the eventual outcome.

ACTUAL EVENT

(-) Negative   **(+) Positive**

-30 -20 -15 -10 -5   **0 +5 +10 +15 +20 +30**

I would consider an incident to be positive or negative based upon multiple factors. Our intentions, expectations, emotions, and conditioned responses propel the potentially neutral event to either a plus or a minus evaluation. We act accordingly. As we saw in the case of Kim's response to Jack Canfield's presentation, people can be involved in the same event and come away with completely different interpretations of what actually occurred. It all depends upon how you individually perceive your reality.

The idea is to live between the minus tens and the plus tens instead of the extreme minus thirties and plus thirties. The former range prevents you from experiencing wide swings to your negative and positive boundaries. You arrest the frustration that comes with scaling high peaks and then plunging down into deep, dark, painful valleys. That ride can be exhilarating and at the same time physically, emotionally, and mentally exhausting. Journeys to the outer limits can erode your ability to reason rationally and look at events objectively. In retrospect, we might conclude that things never are as good or as bad as they might seem or as we create and interpret them.

Let's say that you are anticipating the weekend visit of a longtime dear friend who you haven't seen in many years. You are thrilled about seeing this person, and your expectations are that you both are going to have a great time. You anticipate that you will talk about old times and reminisce about shared experiences. You will get caught up, hang out, and renew your enduring relationship.

In preparation for the visit, you clean up the house, get the yard manicured, wash the car, and stock the refrigerator with exotic food and expensive wines. You put fragrant flowers in the guest room, fresh sheets on the guest bed, and clean, fluffy towels in the guest bathroom.

You arrive early at the airport and pace back and forth excitedly in the baggage claim area foreseeing an exhilarating couple of days with this treasured friend. It is going to be terrific. You can't wait to see him or her walking down the concourse. This potential neutral event is now being pushed out to a plus thirty by your expectations before any supporting evidence suggests such a positive score. You are setting yourself up for a potential crash and disappointment.

You meet your friend, exchange a hug, and carry his or her heavy bags to your car while he or she is on a cell phone returning a variety of personal and business calls that came in during the flight to visit you. Your friend seems tired from the trip, along with looking a bit older and heavier than you remembered. And whoa, he or she just lit up a cigarette in your car with the windows up. Did he or she smoke before? Plus thirty just plummeted to a plus ten, but there is still time to bump it up to your expectations. You still have hope for the remaining time together. It is just a slight setback, but the excitement is still there.

The weekend passes slowly. It crawls by as you find it difficult to find common, familiar ground. You argue about politics and religion. Your friend never picks up the tab for anything. And you're being eaten out of cupboard, pantry, and refrigerator! Time has definitely put different interpretations on what you thought were shared experiences and memories. By the time you drop off your friend at the airport on Sunday evening, you calibrate the total experience as a minus twenty, maybe even a minus thirty or beyond. The event held so much promise, but you were silently relieved to see it end.

Of course, we could reverse the scenario and turn a minus fifteen into a plus ten. In either case, to help you avoid the roller coaster of emotions, I recommend that you consider viewing the actual event from the starting point of a neutral zero, let the experience unfold, and then—with more reasonable expectations—respond with an open-ended attitude about how it is going. This will allow you to respond with the appropriate level of emotion and thus avoid extreme highs and lows. In the example I gave, the intention was to have an enjoyable time, but there are no guarantees. Your unilateral, exaggerated expectations caused the problems.

This philosophy may seem like a vanilla way to go through life and contrary to what you are accustomed to. But a strategy such as this keeps events and circumstances in proper perspective. It allows you the opportunity to respond without the wild swings that create stress and unwanted, disappointing, and unproductive reactions. It takes you off the roller coaster and seats you comfortably on a carousel with moderate ups and downs. I am not suggesting that you void yourself of excitement and have no expectations—just keep your expectations between the tens with good intentions. Do what works for you. Create value in your life and do not settle for anything less. You deserve it.

In Viktor Frankl's hallmark book, *Man's Search for Meaning*, he described such a crossroads, which he faced during his incarceration in a Nazi concentration camp. "We who lived in concentration camps can remember the men who walked through the huts comforting others, giving away their last piece of bread. They may have been few in number, but they offer sufficient proof that everything can be taken from a man but one thing: the last of the human freedoms—

to choose one's attitude in any given set of circumstances, to choose one's own way."

Anything that I have encountered in my life pales in comparison to the unimaginable conditions that the concentration camp prisoners encountered. It is humbling to be complaining about the inconveniencies of modern-day life when one reflects on the experiences that Dr. Frankl and countless others endured. "What, no wireless Internet service? You mean the air conditioner will be off for a couple of hours? What's with this slow room service? Traffic is now stalled on I-5 and the commute will take an additional hour. Sorry, but today's show is sold out. My wife, husband, kids, mom, dad, boss . . . just don't get it." Put your life in perspective and act accordingly. Life is good, and you have the ability and resources to make it even better.

What good does it do you to scurry around and gather self-serving additional evidence that the encroaching tide has turned against you? None at all! You may not be able to alter entirely the velocity of the flow of the unwanted current of circumstances coming toward you, but you can change your perspective about the temporary setback and not be so invested in feeling bad. Dial yourself into a more positive frequency that propels you toward your vision and aspirations. This will break you free from the tyranny of past conditioning or stored unconscious negative core beliefs and emotions.

Let me put into perspective for you in a somewhat subjective manner what you are up against regarding the possibilities of choosing appropriate or inappropriate feelings and emotions. It depends largely upon circumstances, as well as how you have been conditioned and/or have chosen to respond.

In her book *Outsmart Your Brain: How to Make Success Feel Easy*, Marcia Reynolds inventories emotions and feelings in specific categories. One of her premises is that our emotions influence our thoughts, and if we remain aware, we can make better choices and not be held hostage to emotions that spiral us downward into a deep and dark hole, or away from more productive thoughts and actions. For example, if you feel angry, that feeling can escalate into other thoughts and the further emotions of fury, rage, hatred, etc., all of which will separate and isolate you from more positive choices and thoughts. You get vacuumed down potentially into a devastating spiral that prevents you from choosing alternative thoughts that will be more positive and productive and that will assist you in solving the dilemma that you created.

This model suggests that you have a wide range of responses that will trigger thoughts that will initiate actions that will serve you and others more positively. You can make better choices for yourself if you stay aware and break old patterns consciously.

Remember, emotions are powerful. They are triggered by thoughts. Whatever the emotion you are feeling, it is an indicator of what you are thinking. Positive emotions reflect positive thoughts and will then trigger additional positive thoughts. Negative emotions reflect negative thoughts and will then trigger additional negative thoughts. You must perpetuate what it is that will bring you joy and gratitude. You are in charge of any cycle of thoughts and emotions you experience. I'll say it again: You make the choice.

EXERCISES

Look at each emotion printed in bold and then circle or highlight the accompanying emotion(s) that consistently define you in situations when you are expressing the initial bold-print emotion. For example, your initial anger may escalate into further destructive and nonproductive emotions and thoughts, such as hatred or contempt. Answer each italicized question that follows the categories.

Anger: fury, outrage, hatred, resentment, exasperation, annoyance, irritation, vengeance, belligerence, rebellion, resistance, envy, superiority, defiance, contempt, repulsion, offense, distrustfulness, cynicism, wariness, concern, apprehension

> *What would be an alternative response, if your response was negative, that would serve you better and lead you to a better result?*

Fear: nervousness, dread, worry, apprehension, anxiety, stress, restlessness, fright, obsession

> *What would be an alternative response that would serve you better and lead you to a better result?*

Disheartened: confused, baffled, lost, disoriented, disconnected, trapped, lonely, isolated, sad, grieving, dejected, gloomy, desperate, depressed, devastated, helpless, weak, vulnerable, moody, serious, somber, disappointed, hurt, defective, shy, unloved, abandoned, frail, queasy, weary, tired, burned-out, apathetic, complacent, bored, exhausted, frustrated, grumpy, testy, wound-up

> *What would be an alternative response that would serve you better and lead you to a better result?*

EXERCISES (CONTINUED)

Shame: humiliation, mortification, embarrassment, chagrin, guilt, discomfort, regret, remorse, reflection, sorrow, detachment, aloofness

> *What would be an alternative response that would serve you better and lead you to a better result?*

Surprised: shocked, startled, stunned, amazed, astonished, impressed

> *What would be an alternative response, if your response was negative, that would serve you better and lead you to a better result?*

Impassioned: enthusiastic, excited, aroused, delirious, passionate, confident, bold, eager, optimistic, gratified, proud, gushy

> Think of an experience from your past when you felt impassioned and relive it. Notice the feelings. Store this experience in your data bank so that you can readily retrieve it when you are feeling the opposite.

Happy: joyful, blissful, amused, delighted, triumphant, lucky, pleased, silly, dreamy, enchanted, appreciative, grateful, hopeful, intrigued, interested, engrossed, alive, vivacious

> Think of an experience from your past when you felt happy and relive it. Notice the feelings. Store this experience in your data bank so that you can readily retrieve it when you are feeling the opposite.

Calm: contented, relieved, peaceful, relaxed, satisfied, reserved, comfortable, receptive, forgiving, accepting, loved, serene

EXERCISES (CONTINUED)

Think of an experience from your past when you felt calm and relive it. Notice the feelings. Store this experience in your data bank so that you can readily retrieve it when you are feeling the opposite.

Regard: adoration, admiration, reverence, love, affection, security, respect, friendship, sympathy, compassion, tenderness, generosity

Think of an experience from your past when you felt regard and relive it. Notice the feelings. Store this experience in your data bank so that you can readily retrieve it when you are feeling the opposite.

Answer each of the following questions about appropriately dealing with emotions:

- What drives you to consistently choose this response, and how does it serve you and others?

- What are the consequences for your life if you do not change your auto-response?

- What is your self-determined payoff for continuing to respond in the same manner, getting the same result?

- What will it take to evolve to being able to express a different response that will better your life and the lives of the people you impact?

- Would you rather be right or at peace with yourself and the Universe?

- Recall a time or an event in your past when you achieved a high degree of success or were part of an exciting and positive experience. Perhaps you won an award, held

EXERCISES (CONTINUED)

your newborn for the first time, lost excess weight, or got married. Picture that event in your mind's eye, allow your inner dialogue to talk about the experience, and let your emotions into your awareness. Feel them and allow those feelings to expand as if you were actually in that past experience. Those are the emotions that you want to anchor with your affirmations and visualizations. Go back and repeat the process with another event or experience from the past. The more repetitions, the better you will become.

• This time, project forward. Think about something positive and valuable that you want to experience in the future. Affirm that you have it already. See yourself enjoying it and let the feelings and emotions that accompany the affirmation and the visualization seep into your awareness. Keep repeating this process. Change your affirmation and visualization if the emotions and feelings are mundane. Inject more exciting words into your affirmations and enhance the pictures.

REVIEW

TOOL TIME

*A determined soul will do more with a rusty monkey wrench than
a loafer will accomplish with all the tools in a machine shop.*

—ROBERT HUGHES
AUSTRALIAN ART CRITIC, WRITER, AND BROADCASTER

It is time to set your sights, zero in, take decisive action, and place
in motion (or continue) your journey to get more of what you aspire
to. Call in the troops, your assistant, mentor, savior, source, partner,
leader, or guide. Bring them along on your journey to create and live a
customized life because you may need some fuel stops and recharging
along the way. Today's sixty is yesterday's forty, and you are in for a
long ride no matter when and where you launch. Use *Aspire* as your
reference guide, or anything else that captures your attention if you
have a desire to do it your way.

Everything that you need is inside of you. Allow open-minded
wonderment—not strict obedience—direct you. Stay open to other

considerations and do what works for you at this time of your life. It is your life—make it remarkable. Make it yours.

Allegiance to a guru and devotion to ancient disciplines pale in comparison to the results that you are able to achieve when you are connected to your higher purpose. It all works at a wondrous level when you choose to be accountable. What is essential is that you get started and manifest the life that you desire and deserve. Open yourself to the unlimited possibilities.

You have at your immediate disposal a built-in manifestation toolbox. It is staring back at you in the mirror—it's you. It is filled with everything that you will ever need to construct the life that you aspire to have. It has been inside of you the entire time. It is your life for the remainder of your life. People will come and go, but you are always present and on board on your personal journey. Begin by opening all of the pullout drawers in the toolbox that is you, and discover what has been issued to you upon arrival. The future is you and the Universe!

Let's review and see what is inside. The first drawer in the toolbox that is you contains accountability instructions. Do not proceed until you are wide-awake and ready to take responsibility for your life; otherwise, you will be bumping into walls. You cannot sleepwalk through life and experience the results that we have been discussing and that are waiting to be drawn into your life. This process needs your full attention.

Drawers two and three are filled with challenges and methodologies to declare what you want more of and to lay down a solid foundation of core beliefs and assumptions. This is your launching pad. Make it stable and unwavering. If you are not accelerating toward what you desire to be, do, and have, or what you desire to start, stop, and continue, then make the appropriate adjustments. Life is not a sentence of condemnation, but rather a continuous adventure filled with mysteries, wonderment, joy, and gratitude. You are not destined to live a life under another's thumb.

No passing the buck or finger-pointing, though. There is a shredder and compactor available to eliminate those core beliefs and ego-driven motives that are not serving you. Be courageous and rid yourself of those issues and reactions that are preventing you from receiving the joy and gratefulness that you desire and deserve. Break the broom out of the closet and sweep your path clear. Remove those annoying obstacles.

Pull out drawers four through eleven and discover a wide assortment of fascinating multifunctional tools, techniques, and mechanisms for creating more of your self-determined life. They will propel you toward your future. You will build a sturdy launch platform for broadcasting powerful energy-charged thoughts, pictures, and emotions. Some of the tools might feel a bit awkward at first, but with practice, your skill level and proficiency will improve. Stay on the bus and experiment. Be the driver and the tour director, not just a passenger sitting passively in the rear. Be as courageous as civil rights leader Rosa Parks was and claim what is rightfully yours. She did what was the right thing for her and became the tipping-point for many others. Why not you?

Poke around in your kit full of tools and techniques that you will find useful as you learn how to become your own "handy person"; stop outsourcing your life to others whom you believe have the answers. It is all there in your toolbox waiting for your proper implementation. Once you learn which end is up, where the energy source is located, and how to adjust to and be comfortable with this wireless system, you will manifest the process with perfect connectivity.

Along with the tool kit is your manual (this book and many others that you choose, plus your own intuition)—the instructions that you will need in order to construct the life that you aspire to create.

You decide what you want to have, determine the blueprint that is best suited for you, and let the flow of energy begin to construct and implement the desired outcome. Do it now, in the present!

It is time to put down the remote, get off the couch, open drawer number one, and get started. Don't be concerned about any leftover or redundant parts on the floor after whatever you are building is fully assembled. It is an oversupplied and abundant world—just pass them along for others to use and enjoy.

I wish you good fortune. Have a safe and exciting journey. Include in your travel bag your internal toolbox, rechargeable batteries, and a full roll of duct tape. You should always have a good supply of all three, just in case you get amnesia about your capabilities, your life starts to lose momentum, or parts begin to unravel. Fasten your seat belt tight across your lap and turn those electronic devices to the "off" position. In the unlikely event of an emergency, put on your oxygen mask first. The person next to you will figure it out sooner or later. It's going to be an exciting and rewarding trip. Leave in your wake a better world, having lived your life fully conscious and fully accountable, and having made a positive contribution. This will be your legacy.